What others are saying about

God's Peace in Your Home

We have been in professional counseling for over two years with several different counselors. None were able to explain the origin of our anger. Before we finished the third section of your insights, we became aware that at last we found answers we had been searching for. Your down-to-earth application of scripture helped us to see how our sin had been passed from our parents, to us, then to our children. We praise God for your proclaiming His life changing words of deliverance.
Catherine Rinne, R.N.
Medical Supervisor

Wow! I find it so powerful - certainly helpful information for the family. I especially appreciated the way you framed anger and conflict as positive vehicles to growth and resolution. Your use of personal scenarios and making yourself so transparent just adds a special genuineness to the total package.
Dr. Marsha Meyer, Ph.D.
Psychologist

It's loaded with information. I'd read sections and go back and reread it. I'd highlight and go back and scan my highlights. It's a very valuable tool for singles, couples, families, churches and Bible studies.
Linda Miller, R.N.
Lay counselor

It was so good. I did have to fight the urge to hang on to the draft copy. I often got so caught up in the content of the book I forgot I was supposed to be offering suggestions. I loved your use of stories; they illustrated your points well. Some illustrated your weaknesses, some illustrated your strengths. I thought it was a perfect balance.

Rhonda Rhea
Author, Speaker,
Mother of five

Reading this has been so good for me. I gained a deeper understanding of the dynamics of my own childhood history and more of an understanding of our marriage struggles. It also challenged me to keep doing the deep heart work needed to continue to walk in truth.

Patti Smith
Marriage/Family Counselor

This should be a must read book for every couple contemplating marriage.

College student

This book would make an excellent text for a Christian college classroom. It contains insightful and practical ideas for enhancing today's family and individual needs relating to anger. Whether for personal or academic purposes, you will profit from this book.

Dr. Michael Firmin, Ph.D.
Chair, Department of Psychology
Cedarville University, Ohio

Chuck's book will be a tremendous resource for the church. It helped me with anger in my own life with a perspective that's a breath of fresh air to someone who is hurting inside. When I share with people I'm counseling, their response has been, "That's what I need."

Dr. Clay Bowlin
Senior Pastor

This is probably the most powerful book I have ever read apart from the Bible! The word picture that came to me was "disassemble." This was letting God speak to me as He disassembled my life for inspection just like a mechanic would disassemble an engine. It has ministered very deeply to me! I felt very much disassembled but God has forgiven me and continues to forgive me! And, He is in the rebuilding process. It has given me so many, many answers that I wish I would have **known** and **understood** thirty or forty years ago!

Glenn
Father of seven

GOD'S PEACE IN YOUR HOME

GOD'S PEACE IN YOUR HOME

TEN WAYS TO REDUCE ANGER IN RELATIONSHIPS

Dr. Chuck Lynch

Special features

Anger reduction keys
Small group study questions

ISBN-13: 9780692652763
ISBN-10: 0692652760

DEDICATION

It is with great joy that I dedicate

this book to our daughters,

DeeDee Lynch Neir

and

Michelle Lynch Peterson.

God has greatly used both of them

to prepare me to write this book.

I now share our story

with their full blessing.

A BIG THANKS!

THERE ARE NOT enough words to thank the hundreds who have allowed me to identify and address biblically the most common sources of anger and frustration in their families.

I am deeply grateful to the Living Foundation Ministries staff who transcribed hundreds of hand written pages into an intelligible manuscript and to the scores of friends and professionals who critiqued the manuscript and made valuable suggestions.

Words alone are not adequate to thank Linda Hight, who tirelessly supervised the many details, adding her own polish to the manuscript and exhibited extra patience with me in the process. A big thanks to Rachel Adcock for the great job on the final editing. We are grateful to Adrian Fonseca Sánchez in Seville, Spain for the book cover design.

I will always be grateful to our daughters, DeeDee and Michelle, for what God taught me through their growing up years in our home.

Faithfully standing in my balcony and cheering me on at every turn is my dear wife, Linda.

And most of all, I thank God for the strength, insight and vision He gave His servant to record His work in the lives of so many people who were then able to help and encourage others. To Him be honor and glory forever.

Chuck Lynch

TABLE OF CONTENTS

INTRODUCTION

GOD'S PEACE IN YOUR HOME

"THE BIBLE IS full of wise counsel on parenting," declared the pastor to a packed Father's Day Sunday morning congregation. I glanced down at my Bible that I read through every year and thought, "Somehow, I must have missed them."

Yes, King Solomon provided wise counsel in the book of Proverbs. But, then I quickly surveyed in my mind the 27 books in the New Testament and I could only come up with two specific passages on parenting and each one is basically a repeat of the other with some added emphasis.

If God could sit down with you over a cappuccino and share just one thing to avoid at all costs in your parenting what would He say? "Fathers, (I add mothers, too) do not provoke your children to anger so that they lose heart and quit trying" (Col 3:21; Eph. 6:4). That's it! But what does that mean?

Provoking or exasperating means "to habitually nag at, to irritate." The Greek construction of these verses literally means "do not keep on nagging or provoking." And God might just lean toward you for emphasis and state, "This is not advice, it is a command."

Why such a stern warning? The habit of stimulating anger in your kids can result in them losing heart, becoming discouraged, shutting down emotionally or just giving up. Again, it literally means that it could result in them continuing to be discouraged for life!

HOW IS IT DONE?

Over the decades of helping parents deal with conflict with their kids, many of the most common sources of anger and frustration keep coming up:

- Over-protection
- Favoritism
- Rejection
- Criticism
- Selfishness
- Impatience
- Discipline in anger
- Perfectionism
- Hurts
- Unresolved conflict

True, anger is the most destructive emotion there is in relationships. But anger can also have a positive side. It can reveal needs. Anger is an emotion that speaks up for a need. What can happen if a legitimate need is revealed and met?

PEACE! GOD'S PEACE!

You are about to further understand how you can use legitimate anger in your kids to identify a need in your relationships that God wants to meet for your benefit and His glory (Matthew 5:16). You are not just going to be told to stop the negative pattern. But you will be able to discover what the real need is and how to meet it in a very practical fashion.

This book was first published in Latin America in 2005. In one large church in Barquisimeto, Venezuela, Francisco and Irma have led over 5,000 people through this book in small groups. Whole families have been rescued from the destructive pain of fighting and arguing that robbed God's peace from their homes.

The application of these biblical principles will bring a much greater peace than you can imagine in any relationship. Now you're ready to welcome a member of the family. Anger. Yes, anger.

Dr. Chuck Lynch

SECTION I
MEET AN OLD FRIEND OF THE FAMILY

CHAPTER 1

ANGER, A FRIEND OF THE FAMILY

"Welcome them as friends"

(JAMES 1:2)

MY FATHER WAS an alcoholic. He made good money but spent it on his addiction. I know what it's like to stack pieces of bread like pancakes and pour brown gravy over them to fill me up. What meat we had went fast between my two brothers and me.

Fifteen hundred miles away in Winchester, Indiana, lived a couple with no children. Bernard worked with my dad years before. Bernard and his wife, Audrey, sent my mom a little extra money to make ends meet. Why did they do this? They were friends of the family. Even years later, when I would visit them, Bernard always slipped me a little gas money. Why? Because they were friends of the family. These friends met our needs.

There is another "friend," usually an unwelcome friend, with a slightly different role. His name is Anger. He, too, can meet a need in any relationship. You may think, "With friends like this who needs enemies?" How can such a destructive emotion be a friend? It can. This friend can have a unique and beneficial purpose for your family. I agree with Dr. Gary Oliver, the executive director of the Center for Marriage and Family Studies at John Brown University, "In Christian circles, not enough has

3

been written on the positive side of anger. Anger has tremendous potential for good" (p.283).

Dr. Oliver estimates that 90% of the Christians he has polled view anger from an almost exclusively negative perspective (p.278). Psychologist and author, Dr. Harriet Learner, explains two possible reasons for this, "Nothing, no nothing, will block the awareness of anger so effectively as guilt and self-doubt" (p.5). It is true that of all the God-given emotions, anger is the most challenging.

I believe if you can accept the fact that anger is a God-given emotion and learn to use the positive benefits, you can have an incredible quality of life. This friend of the family can be used to bring God's peace into your home.

THE RED LIGHT NOTIFIER

A blizzard had unleashed its white-out fury just days before I was to present a seminar in Arnold, Nebraska. Although the roads had just been plowed they were still barely passable. I was sure the seminar would be cancelled. However, the hearty Nebraskan ranchers and farmers plowed their snow-drifted lanes and opened the narrow two-lane highways to travel. They also shoveled the walks around the host church. Despite the snow, attendance the first night of the seminar was unbelievably high.

The next day, Linda and I began our precarious trek from our host's farm to the church in town to begin an all-day session of the seminar. As we drove through two-foot drifts to reach the main highway, the red lights on my dashboard lit up. The power steering died. I fought every turn. The power brakes failed. Snow blocked the exit ramps so there was nowhere to go. A feeling of panic swept over me. The motor temperature began rising despite the freezing temperature. Something was seriously wrong.

We barely made the ten-mile trek into town. As we pulled up to the church, the motor died. I popped the hood and found the motor packed with snow from driving through snowdrifts. I realized that the snow had caused the main belt that powers most everything to slip off its pulley. The red lights had been my first warning, my notifier that something was wrong.

ANGER - MY NOTIFIER

Anger can serve the same function as the red light on the dashboard of the car. It is designed to notify you of a problem that must be addressed, and addressed soon. Anger, like the red light, never *fixes* anything. Anger is a way of saying, "Hey! Notice my need." Like psychologist and author, Dr. Les Carter, would say, it's an emotion that "speaks up" for personal needs (p. 28). It is a God-given tool that signals something is not right and needs to change. Just as physical pain tells you to take your hand off the hot stove, emotional pain serves the same purpose.

The writer of Psalm 42 used emotional pain to discover a need. He explains, "Why are you cast down, O my soul: And why are you disquieted within me?" (Ps. 42:5a). He does not beat himself up for feeling down in the dumps but traces those feelings back to a need. In his case, he had lost hope in God and was having a trust crisis. His despair notified him of his need to restore his hope in God.

If you ignore the red light of anger when it notifies you of hurt, fear or frustration, life will continue, but like my disabled car, the quality of performance will be less than desirable. In time, a breakdown will occur with very costly consequences.

Psychiatrist and author, Dr. Paul Meier, feels that part of the cost of the improper handling of anger could cause up to 95% of psychological depressions. He is also convinced that just the *fear* of acknowledging the anger that is being held in is a primary cause of anxiety (p. 7). Conflict is one of the consequences that comes when angry feelings are ignored. Guess what? Conflict can be just as beneficial as anger.

BENEFITS OF CONFLICT

Anger and conflict both serve as friendly notifiers that you have a need that must be addressed. Properly handled, conflict can serve as a doorway to better relational harmony. Why? Because conflict, like anger, can reveal a need that God wants to meet for your benefit and His glory (Matt. 5:16).

Conflict has several benefits. First, conflict may reveal the ineffective ways you are attempting to get your own needs met. Solomon wisely observed, "There is a way that seems right to a man, but the ends are the ways of death" (Prov.14:12). Habits or behaviors that seems normal or right to you can actually lead to destruction of a relationship. Conflict will reveal that need.

Ramona knew that first hand. Roger, Ramona's husband, had just finished an all- night shift at work. He, his wife and two kids came for family counseling. As they drove home after our session, Roger's all-night shift caught up with him and he began to nod off. Ramona yelled at him to pull over and let someone else drive. He stubbornly refused. The kids joined the parental yelling match.

At our next session, I asked Ramona what need she was trying to meet by yelling at Roger. She looked at me, then looked at her husband and dropped her eyes. She did not want to do this. It made her feel vulnerable to reveal her heartfelt need. Her anger was safe, but revealing her heart was not. She struggled. In a soft voice she said, "I was scared. I thought we would all be killed and it seemed like he didn't care!"

"Have you tried to tell Roger you were scared?" I asked. She paused, "No... I just get angry with him when he does something like that and I just go off on him."

"Has that ever been effective?" I probed further.

She exhaled deeply, "No, I guess not."

"Would you turn to Roger and tell him about your fear?"

In hushed, halting tones, and for the first time in their 12 years of marriage, Ramona quietly shared her fears. She was able to tell Roger the yelling did not mean she didn't love him. Ramona's fear had shifted into anger, and it came out in bitter, cutting remarks that deflected attention away from her needs to feel safe.

"Roger, were you aware of your wife's fears?" I asked him.

Blinking back tears he said, "I just thought she didn't like me . . . I mean . . . like she hated me and her screaming only proved it."

Roger's two children sat on the couch watching their parents interact in a heart-to-heart way for the first time. Anger-based conflict had revealed Ramona's need to feel safe and secure.

Many fights in the Christian family are over legitimate needs that people are attempting to meet in an unacceptable way. Conflict, like anger, can notify you that the behavior you are demonstrating, which seems right to you, if continued, will end in the ways of death (Prov. 14:12). In a relationship, this can mean separation or worse, divorce.

WELCOME A FRIEND OF THE FAMILY

It is believed that James, the half-brother of Jesus, was the first person to write a book in what we know today as the New Testament.

In the book of James, one of the first issues that James deals with is how to face trials. However, he applies a strange twist to how we normally think of trials. "Consider it all joy, my brethren, when you encounter various trials" (James 1:2) or, as J. B. Phillip paraphrases it, "When all kinds of trials crowd into your lives, my brothers, welcome them as friends."

Friends? Yes. Friends. Why? James explains the personal benefits trials or conflicts can have in your life (James 1:3-4). You may have a legitimate need and a conflict's first benefit is to reveal that need and the ineffective way in which you have been trying to meet that need. Remember that arguments or "fights" are usually designed to fulfill some unmet need. Through the trial, you can uncover the need and find a more effective way to meet that need. Conflict can do something else for you in addition to revealing an unmet need; it can create understanding.

CREATE UNDERSTANDING

The second benefit of conflict, when channeled appropriately, is that it can lead to a deeper understanding between believers and could potentially serve as a basis for a positive change. This could usher in the peace you so deeply desire.

When Roger, Ramona and their kids came in for counseling, I asked their son, Travis, what he was feeling and thinking when his folks had their big blow up in the car. He glared at me, then, at his dad, then, back at me as if to say, "Do I have to?" I nodded.

Then, after a few moments, he explained that he, too, thought they were all going to be killed that night. He even pictured them dying on a hospital gurney.

"Would you share that with your dad?" I asked.

"I just did!" he retorted.

"No, look at him and in a gentle, respectful way, tell your dad about your own fears."

He took a deep breath and said, "Dad, I thought we were all going to die that night. Man, I was scared stiff!"

I wish I could have video-taped Roger's face. His usual self-defensiveness melted. In a quiet, sincere voice he said, "I'm sorry, I . . . I didn't know you were so scared. I just thought you wanted to fight, too. I wasn't thinking! All I heard was disrespect. I didn't know you were afraid." Then he said, "I guess I did not understand."

Understand. The Apostle Peter gives insight about the importance of understanding in relationships. At the end of his life, having been a husband and an apostle, Peter revealed a relational key for the home in general and marriage in particular: "You husbands likewise, live with your wives in an understanding way, as with a weaker vessel, since she is a woman; and grant her honor as a fellow heir of the grace of life, so that your prayers may not be hindered" (I Peter 3:7).

Husbands are commanded to live with their wives in a knowledgeable, intelligent way. One small problem: often we do not *know* that way so instead we experience *conflict.* Now we can welcome conflict as a friend if it helps us to learn our mate's needs and enables us to grow in understanding them. Under the guidance of God's Holy Spirit, we can make the appropriate changes.

And what if we don't address these needs? Simple. Your "Christian" home, family, marriage could disintegrate before your very eyes just as it does in the rest of the world. Your status as a believer does not invalidate sin's law of cause and effect. The Apostle Paul sternly warns, "Do not be deceived, God is not mocked; for whatever a man sows, this he will also reap" (Gal. 6:7). Nevertheless, conflict and anger can bring about deeper understanding and appropriate positive change if you are mature enough to be teachable and make the change.

LOVE LANGUAGE

A third benefit of anger-based conflict is that it may alert you to the need to change the way you express love to one another. Dr. Gary Chapman's incredible book, *The Five Love Languages*, points out that each of us has our own love language, our own way of feeling loved. He describes five of the most common ways love is expressed: acts of service, gifts, quality time, words of affirmation and physical touch.

A prominent politician told me that he would feel loved if his wife would do just one nice thing as he left for work each morning. It wasn't until both of them sat in my office for marriage counseling that his wife found out this was an important part of his love language. He felt unloved. She felt unappreciated. They were both angry. They fought over other issues, but their conflict revealed these two needs. I asked him to tell his wife one thing she could do that would help him feel loved.

Almost too embarrassed to say it, he blurted out, "Just stand at the door and wave goodbye to me in the morning." He then dropped his head, expecting a disparaging answer to his simple request. Her eyes shot wide open and she stammered, "I . . . I didn't know that meant so much to you."

I turned to her and asked if she would be open to doing that as often as it was reasonably possible. Still in wide-eyed amazement, she said, "Sure."

Conflict can teach us how to express Christ-like love and how to receive love. Even Jesus did not leave the love language issue to guesswork on our part. He summarized His own love language this way: "If you love Me," He simply declared, "you will keep My commandments" (John 14:15).

Conflict that is welcomed as a friend and dealt with biblically can educate us about how to express love and to be loved. Conflict can also have a fourth benefit. It can result in glorifying God.

CONFLICT FOR HIS GLORY

All believers fight. They may not yell, scream, hit or throw things, although I know believers who have. Instead they will use sarcasm, pout, withdraw, criticize, ignore, manipulate, control, shame, utilize guilt trips, shift blame, deny and compare unfavorably. These are just a few ways both believers and nonbelievers fight. How, you may ask, can this type of un-Christ-like behavior glorify God? It is not the sinful behavior that radiates praise back to God. It is something else that is related to the conflict.

An angry conflict can reveal a wrong pattern of behavior that may have been entrenched for years becoming a deep-seated habit. Others may even characterize you by this behavior (or manner of dealing with anger). It becomes part of you, and it is wrong. Have you ever heard someone refer to their mate, boss or child by saying, "He has a short fuse?" In reality, he may have a short fuse because he is full of bitterness. Two of our Lord's disciples, James and John, were known for their tempers. They were called the "sons of thunder" (Mark 3:17). They had no qualms about expressing their anger. They even requested permission to command fire to come down from heaven and consume some Samaritans who had rejected them (Luke 9:54).

This book will help you to identify and correct ten of the most common sources of anger that I have observed throughout our counseling ministry. Our primary focus will be the family; whether it is a traditional, blended or single-parent home. Here is a list of the top ten sources for anger:

- Over-protection - Controlling
- Favoritism
- Rejection
- Criticism
- Selfishness
- Impatience
- Discipline
- Perfectionism
- Un-forgiveness
- Irresponsibility

When a person changes radically, others are amazed because God has taken control of some of these ten sinful relational patterns. Friends and family press to understand what happened. After hearing how submission to Christ, confession and repentance has resulted in a changed life, believers exclaim, "Praise the Lord." God is indeed glorified!

Anger can be an unusual doorway to harmony and may be one indication of conflict's presence. Welcome anger as a friend of the family. View your problems and/or conflicts as opportunities to grow in your family relationship and bring God's peace into your home. It will help you pinpoint where you are in your relationships just as an x-ray aids your doctor in pinpointing a physical injury. Conflict, characterized by the presence of anger, can serve as a motivator for growth in at least three areas: words, actions and attitudes.

THE WORDS WE SAY

How can anger serve the family? It can pinpoint the words we speak that destroy the peace in our homes. I learned this the hard way with my own daughter.

I had been invited to speak at a men's retreat on the topic of "How to Build Family Harmony." As I was packing the car in the driveway, my oldest daughter, DeeDee, walked by briskly. I stuck out my arm to stop her so we could just chat awhile. She firmly brushed aside my extended arm and disappeared into the house. Wondering what that was all about, I put down my briefcase and followed her upstairs to her room. The door was closed. That was a hint. I knocked. No answer. I gently knocked again. Silence.

As I slowly opened the door, there she sat cross-legged on her bed with her back pressed against the antique oak headboard. I sat down on the edge of her bed.

"Would you be open to telling me what the problem is?"

Silence.

"Did I do something to hurt you?"

More silence.

After various attempts to penetrate her defensive wall of silence, I said, "Would you be open to at least praying for me so that God would let me know how I messed up?"

"It wouldn't do any good," came the sharp retort.

Ouch! My heart sank.

I reached over and grasped her hand, gently squeezed it, stood up and feeling emotionally beaten, I left her room.

As I walked down the hall the familiar sense of failure - an old "friend" of mine, broke into my thoughts. Here I was on my way to enthusiastically tell men how to be dynamic fathers and reduce anger in their homes; meanwhile my own daughter was not talking to me.

Glancing over my shoulder, I thought, "What business do I have to challenge these men to build harmony in their homes when my own daughter is alienated from me?" "Worse yet," I thought, "She has lost any confidence she may have had in God." Later I learned the painful truth. I had told her to do something earlier that day, but out of my own impatience, I used a harsh tone of voice. I often confused harshness with firmness.

DeeDee's angry response to me may not have been right. That falls into *her* own circle of responsibility. Still my harsh words had stimulated her anger. That fell into my part of responsibility. I was guilty of "exasperating" her (Eph. 6:4) and was clearly wrong. DeeDee's anger revealed to me the amount of hurt in my harsh words. Her response revealed my need to soften my tone of voice, to be the gentle man God intended. How soon I had forgotten that only about 7% of communication is made up of the words, 38% is the tone of voice and 55% is body language!

I've never forgotten that day. Yes, I have failed on numerous occasions since, but the intent of my heart from that day on was to watch my words as well as my tone of voice and accompanying body language. I grieved that I hurt my daughter but her anger revealed my need to shift from harsh words to gentle words that are seasoned with grace (Col. 4:6).

Angry reactions from others can notify you that your destructive words need to be changed to constructive words. Ephesians 4:29 has pierced my conscience many times: "Let no unwholesome word proceed from your mouth but only such a word as is good for edification according to the need of the moment, that it may give grace to those who hear." The word "*unwholesome*" refers to something rotten or decaying, such as rotten fish. You are not to allow any rotten words to proceed out of your mouth, but only those words that build up a person word-by-word or brick-by-brick into a beautiful Christ-like structure.

I once asked a member of an audience to help me make this very point. I took four small cardboard brick-sized boxes, positioned them on a chair next to us and made a square. Then I asked him to stand next to me and pick up each "brick" one at a time and toss them across the room to an empty chair about ten feet away. His goal was to reproduce the same square configuration on the seat of the distant chair. He could not go over and place them on the chair, he had to stand next to me and throw them across the room. Something became immediately apparent. Thrown bricks do not work as well as hand-placed bricks! Your well-placed words will be received by the listener "like apples of gold in settings of silver" (Prov. 25:11). But your harsh words will eat away inside someone's heart and the rottenness will come out as anger, destroying any hope of peace at home (Eph. 6:4). Careless words, like tossing bricks, *never* produce a godly design.

Harsh words also stir up anger. By contrast, gentle words appropriately placed, turn away wrath (Prov.15:1). How do we know gentle words are God's words of choice? We know because gentleness is a fruit of the Holy Spirit (Gal. 5:22-23). It is the gentle answer that greatly reduces anger in a relationship. It brings God's peace into your home. Harsh words are usually the result of anger.

Anger can reveal other kinds of words that need to be changed in order to experience God's peace in your home. Griping should be changed to appropriate appreciation (Phil 2:14). Unconstructive criticism should be replaced by constructive criticism balanced with praise (I Cor. 11:1, 17). Critical words can eat away any meaningful relationship. Criticism is one of the four most destructive anger-causing elements leading to divorce. The other three elements are defensiveness, contempt, and withdrawal.

An angry response from others, as wrong as it is, can reveal the need in you to change your words and thus do your part to reduce the anger. The presence of anger can effectively reveal a need to make a major change in your choices and use of words. It can also reveal something that can be equally hurtful - your actions.

THE ACTIONS WE DISPLAY

Anger can be used to pinpoint areas where you need to grow with regard to the actions you display. Actions can include entrenched habits we have mentioned earlier, like: over-protection, controlling, favoritism, rejection, criticism, selfishness, impatience, unhealthy discipline, perfectionism, un-forgiveness or irresponsibility.

Jill grew up in a religious home that was characterized by a lot of religious ritual but little emphasis on a relationship with a personal God. Any similarities between the regular Sunday morning church ritual and the day-to-day dynamics of the home were purely accidental. Jill's father was authoritarian instead of being a servant- leader in the home. He was opinionated, controlling and a rage-aholic. He was stingy toward the family but denied himself nothing. By contrast, her mother was a pleaser, a peacemaker, very compliant, shy, hardworking and very verbally and physically affectionate in the family. She was a compliant pleaser and what Dr. Harriet Learner would describe in her book, *The Dance of Anger*, as "an emotional service station" (p. 7) for her husband who was an angry controller.

Jill married after working only two years following high school graduation. It was not until her twenty-fifth wedding anniversary that she came to my office.

"I don't know what's wrong with me," were her opening words. "Lately I've begun to be so impatient, just seething inside. I don't even want to be around my family. It's just not me."

"Is there a particular family member that you find yourself wanting to avoid?" I inquired.

"I just shouldn't feel this way. I don't like me."

"Who is it you don't want to be around?"

"It's my husband, but he is not a bad person. He's a good provider and he doesn't run around on me. He's the treasurer of our church."

"And this is why you don't want to be around him?" I asked.

"If I just wouldn't get angry, things would be okay."

"What does he do to make you angry? Sometimes, Jill, looking at reality can be scary. But God will only give grace for acknowledging the truth (John 1:14). Your anger is attempting to notify you or your husband of your needs and his needs."

Feeling safe, she began. "Rich has a military background. He's been retired for a few years. Our home just seems to be an extension of the military base. He's controlling, harsh and a perfectionist. Yes, he's a hard worker. He helps certain people but is very selective. He is impatient and rules the home with his anger."

She paused, dropping her voice, "He's not very loving; no touching unless it is for sex, no compassion or kind words." Then in an agitated voice she said, "He gets angry so easily and may even pick a fight with just about anyone. He is very unforgiving, yet he can be so jovial with outsiders. But that's okay. What I need help for is my anger."

"Did I hear you say those behaviors are okay? Like normal?" I inquired.

Her face registered bewilderment with my question.

"He's not the problem. He can't help it. Everyone has problems. He is no worse than anyone else. I'm the problem. It's my anger!" She said.

"Jill, you are angry and you do need to address it biblically. But, do you think that your anger is also alerting you to some needs in your marriage? Again, do you view your husband's behavioral patterns as normal?"

It was then she shared with me that she lived with this same behavior growing up with her dad. *What you and I experience as we grow up is what we tend to think of as normal or acceptable.* Jill did, but her emotions were screaming at her that she was in pain. Her anger was evidence of that pain. This is a positive value of anger. It can notify you not only of the tones of voice and kinds of words that are hurtful, but also of the actions and habits that are wrong and do not reflect the character of God. There is no peace at home without the character of God in the home.

There were five tasks Jill needed to accomplish if she was to be at peace in her heart and her home, whether or not there was any change in her husband.

Admit the presence of anger (notifier).
Acknowledge the offense the anger reveals.
Identify the person(s) responsible for the offense.
Forgive the person(s) causing the offense.
Accept the consequences of the past offense.

Jill took the first step and fulfilled the Apostle Paul's counsel, "Be angry (acknowledge it) yet sin not" (Eph. 4:26). She gave herself permission to feel the anger as a means to honestly acknowledge the years of hurt she experienced. It was easy to pinpoint the offender. With her offender clearly in view, she was willing to use the biblical tool of forgiveness. However, accepting the consequences for the years of hurt and loss was the hard part.

Jill was exhausted, but something changed almost immediately. She clearly saw the needs in her marriage. She was now able to face some very tough issues. You will not be prepared to address the hard issues in a relationship if you do not first process your own anger. Jesus expressed it this way, "Why do you look at the speck that is in your brother's (spouse's) eye, but do not notice the log that is in your own eye? . . . First, take the log out of your own eye and then you will see clearly to take the speck out of your brother's eye" (Matt. 7:3,5).

When Jill realized she had a steel beam of anger in her own eye and removed it through a heart-wrenching time of prayer, she then began to see some things clearly that she had denied for years. Anger drove Jill to the front door of forgiveness and freedom from years of bitterness.

THE ATTITUDES WE CONVEY

Anger not only reveals hurtful words and actions, it also reveals the number one peace killer in the home: our attitudes. A longtime personal friend and prolific writer, Norman Wright, stated in his book, *Crisis Counseling*, "What causes a crisis to become a restrictive, crippling, eternal tragedy rather than a growth-producing experience in spite of the pain? Our attitude" (p. 23).

Jill was the object of Rich's hurtful words and actions, but the thing that devastated her over the years was Rich's overall attitude. Why was this the case? Attitude can be conceptualized as our core belief system. Attitudes are the main control center of all our words and behaviors. King Solomon said you can define a person's character by what emits from his heart or his core belief system, "For as a man thinks within himself (core belief system), so he is (in outward actions) (Prov. 23:7).

Rich's behavior, habits and verbal expressions were bad and they emanated from his attitudes, his core belief center. He validated daily our Lord's words, "But those things and behaviors become a window of the heart and its core attitudes."

There are a number of attitudes that reveal the god of "self" who is at the master control of the heart. Pride, however, wins the prize for the most destructive attitude. It is the father of prejudice, conceit, arrogance, disrespect, selfishness, rejection and control. Hurtful attitudes like pride not only create pain but blunt our desire to correct it. If genuine humility replaces painful pride, this will put God's peace on the fast track to your home.

GET READY

Make a commitment today to yourself to say, "Ouch" when you hurt and give others permission to do so as well. Then get ready to discover the needs behind the anger and explore creative ways to get those needs met. Let's examine together eight of the most common needs I have observed throughout the years that anger has revealed. It will not only benefit your relationships but will give you practical tools to help others in any relational conflict.

ANGER REDUCTION KEYS

1. Welcome anger as the new friend of the family.
2. Accept anger as a normal emotion.
3. Understand what anger is and where it comes from.
4. Pinpoint words, attitudes and actions that need to be changed.
5. Discover the unmet needs in the relationship.
6. Identify the love language of each family member.
7. Use anger to reveal hurts that God wants to heal through forgiveness.
8. Glorify God through your corrected anger patterns.

SMALL GROUP DISCUSSION QUESTIONS

1. How have you seen anger reveal a need that is crying to be met? Were you able to meet it? If so, how did you do it and what was the outcome?

2. What words, attitudes or actions have you discovered over the years that do not produce Christ-like relationships? How did you change them? What were the benefits?

3. In what ways have you seen conflict produce a greater understanding and deepen a relationship?

4. Describe some difficult experiences you have gone through to learn someone else's love language. What were some painful things you went through to communicate your own love language to someone else?

5. What have been some problems that members of your family have gone through to learn how to adjust the words they say, the actions they display or the attitudes they convey?

SECTION II
NUMBER ONE SOURCE OF ANGER

CHAPTER 2

OVER-PROTECTION, A CHILD'S FUEL FOR ANGER

HELEN IS ANGRY. Everyday decisions have been frustrating, but now it is something bigger. Mitch and Helen built their dream house on thirty acres east of town. It had taken hundreds of hours of work for the whole family to clear the building plot of years of neglected undergrowth. It was not easy. But that was not the reason Helen came to see me. It was now interior decorating time.

"I don't know what's wrong with me . . . I just can't make decisions. Do you know how many carpet and drapery samples I have taken home; chosen, ordered, then canceled? Look, I'm 45 years old. I'm a grown woman. What's my problem? My family and the carpet/drapery stores are ready to strangle me." She sighed, turning her head to the side.

Brenda is 25. Her dad is a successful builder. Her mom has been a prominent Christian TV hostess of her own program for years. Brenda was raised in a Christian home. Theologically, she and her parents were as straight as an arrow.

After Brenda turned 22 she met Eric. He was fun-loving and laid-back. Brenda was critical, opinionated, structured, controlling, perfectionistic and highly moral. One day her parents called me in a state of shock and panic. Her mother believed that

Brenda was spending the night at Eric's apartment. Upon checking, their worst fears were confirmed. Months later Brenda and Eric got married. It was rocky from the start. They both eventually came for marriage counseling.

In one of the sessions, Brenda said, "You know why I became sexually involved before I married Eric? He was the very first person I have ever met who liked me for who I was. He did not pressure me with a long list of expectations I had to live up to every time I turned around. It felt good to be me and be liked as well. I foolishly compromised my morals for the first time. It was wrong. I've asked God to forgive me, but I was vulnerable to unconditional love and acceptance that was not based on my performance."

Brenda came from a Christian home with very high morals. Her mother spent hours drilling scripture into Brenda's head. These lectures were called "share times." She was told the right way to feel, eat, think, respond, serve and behave! Her mother unintentionally sought to mold her into the mother's designed image instead of the unique image God had planned for Brenda. Mom's over-protection, control and perfectionism kept Brenda straight in her controlled childhood, but she unintentionally did something else. She set her daughter up for a relational disaster in adulthood.

In contrast, Helen, to use her words, came from a "very wicked and immoral" home. Dad controlled everyone and everything. As a result, Helen was never allowed to make decisions. When she became an adult, guess what? She couldn't make decisions. She would second and third guess everything she did. She was absolutely paralyzed for fear of making a wrong decision. Why? Because she never learned in childhood that you can make a mistake and the world will not come to an end. Helen was having to painfully learn in adulthood what she had not had an opportunity to learn in childhood, due to parental over-protection.

How do you prevent or correct a lifetime of over-protection that fuels the fires of anger both in childhood and adulthood?

Most parents feel they are developing a healthy independence in their children. They may parent as they were parented themselves. However, the way we were raised may not be God's design for a healthy independence in a home of peace. In this chapter we are going to show how an unbiblical and unhealthy dependence occurs resulting in much anger in a child or student. In the next few chapters we will discuss the results of over-protection and how to switch from over-protection to healthy independence.

WALK AWAY INTO ADULTHOOD

My wife, Linda, did not want children when we first got married. Through a series of events God opened her heart and a few years later God gave us DeeDee. The Lamaze childbirth techniques were just becoming popular in the late sixties. I went to the childbirth classes and learned to coach Linda through the delivery. She allowed me to be there for everything.

What an absolute joy it was to have our own baby! The feelings of being a parent were incredible. Just for a fleeting moment we thought how great it would be if DeeDee always remained this warm, cuddly, clingy baby that Linda could nurse for years. We held her tight and savored each moment. Still we knew from day one that it would not last. The grip had to be released. DeeDee would crawl out of our arms and walk away from us into adulthood.

THEY INCREASE – WE DECREASE

When DeeDee was first born we were 100% in control. She was 100% dependent upon us. As she grew and developed, our control decreased and her control increased. It is like a large letter 'X'. The top left represents that we have 100% control. The bottom left of the 'X' represents DeeDee's 100% dependence upon us. As she grows up toward the top right, she takes more control of her life. We, as parents, go from being 100% in control at the top left and gradually reduce our control to "0" on the bottom right. It is a way of God; the children increase in control while we as parents decrease in control. We remain parents in position but our function changes from parent to mentor, consultant and/or best friend. We now relate adult-to-adult.

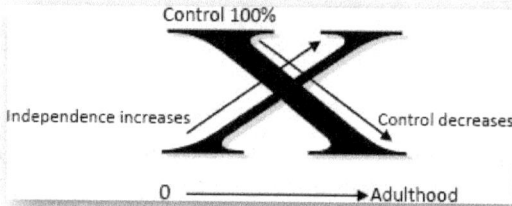

But how is childish immaturity accomplished? Control of the child is never fully released. The child is never given the ultimate responsibility for the direction of his future. Full adult status is rarely achieved. Conversations are usually characterized as parent-to-child instead of adult-to-adult. Healthy independence is never achieved, at least emotionally. The body grows up but the emotions stay behind, very dependent and needy.

Childish immaturity is a distortion of I Cor. 13:10, "When I was a child, I used to speak, think and reason as a child. When I became an adult I *kept my childish perspective and stayed an emotional cripple,* instead of putting away these childish ways."

Psychologist Dr. James Dobson in *Dare to Discipline* describes the results of over-protection as humiliation for the child and an icy atmosphere in the home. This is characterized by rigidity, constant fear, an inability to make decisions, dependent emotional immaturity and a *deep abiding anger.* It can even be a basis for psychosis (p. 11). Abiding anger can become a friend of the family by revealing the need to correct this devastating pattern.

THE OVER-PROTECTED TEEN

What does this over-protected person look like as an adolescent? Many of the following characteristics we describe may not *just* be a direct result of an overprotected student who was micromanaged by parents. However, these are the most common ones I've observed as a result of over-protection. What are at least six characteristics of an over-protected teenager? Let's begin with low self-esteem or low confidence.

LOW CONFIDENCE IN SELF AND GOD

The very opposite of the desired effect occurs as a result of over-protection. Most controlling Christian parents sincerely want their kids to believe in God, obey Him and do the right thing. Their intent is to prevent any harm from coming into their children's lives physically, mentally, emotionally and spiritually. These sincere parents believe they know what is best for their children in all situations. Result? The young person develops an inordinate dependency on them and fails to gain confidence in himself or God through life's struggles. Over-protective parents become their child's "God-substitute." Why trust yourself or God when you have an all-knowing mom and/or dad who make all your decisions for you?

Some controlling parents over-control their student out of fear that if they release their grip, even just a little, the adolescent could ruin their life. Realistically the opposite is likely to happen. They can successfully navigate into adulthood if they are allowed to do some struggling. Failure to allow them to struggle conveys the lie that struggle is bad *and* there are no disappointments in life. Psychologist, Dr. John Friel, points out two results from disallowing struggle. First, it creates a fantasy world for the young adult. Next, it creates an emotional prison for the children and they may never leave home (Adult Children, p. 12). I have seen them leave home unannounced and not speak to their parents or have anything to do with them for years.

An associate pastor asked what he should do about a person formerly in his youth group who is now married. The problem? Without fail, she would call her dad, the senior pastor, and ask him about every decision she or her new husband made. Even the young husband's decisions were not valid until her father validated them.

The family belonged to a good Bible-honoring church. However, both Mom and Dad felt they knew what was best all the time, in every situation. The daughter was born again but grew up emotionally crippled. Like Helen, she second-guessed every decision she made and did not feel peace until her "God-substitute" confirmed her decision. To this day she still has not grown to understand that those who are led by the Spirit of God (not parents) are the sons of God (Rom. 8:14). Receiving counsel is one thing. Needing constant validation of all her decisions is quite another.

Why does this create so much anger in the adolescent? Micromanaging gets translated by the daughter in at least two negative ways. First, she believes something is dreadfully wrong with her and she cannot trust, nor should she trust her own thoughts. This results in anger toward God for making her flawed and unable to make decisions. As this anger grows, she finds herself becoming distanced from God because she feels He is responsible for making her emotionally and intellectually handicapped.

Second, since she feels something must be terribly wrong with her in that she has to be so controlled, she concludes that her mom and dad do not like her. Over-protection can be translated by the child as rejection instead of loving care. Why? Over-protection is rooted in parental fear which conveys rejection, not love.

Children are highly influenced to ultimately accept who they are based on the opinions and practices of others, *especially their parents*. Sadly, young people seek out controlling mates if their parents were over-protective and this dysfunction is perpetrated in the Christian home as it gets passed down generationally (Exodus 20:5). Something else also happens in the church family.

Angry, controlling men who become pastors attract insecure, dependent people. An entire church can become dysfunctionally dependent on its pastor. This pattern is seen in some legalistic, performance-based churches. Strong authoritarian pastors attract to their churches weak, dependent parishioners. Over-protection is thus institutionalized in our religious life and is viewed as normal! Ronald Enroth's book, *Churches That Abuse* addresses this issue.

REJECTION OF RULES, AUTHORITY, VALUES

Why would an adolescent reject the rules, authority and values of his parent or society? One possibility is revenge! He will pick up, evaluate, deem as worthless and turn his back in disdain on these rules.

I was a youth pastor in the 1960's during the hippies' era. One of the most common denominators of the "love children" was an absolute repudiation of the parents' values, rules and authority. Girls traded sex for what they thought was love. Boys traded a deceptive love for sex. Girls used boys; boys used girls.

I once counseled a woman who was taken to the Woodstock Rock Festival two days after she was born. Now in her early thirties she still suffers from the mental, emotional and physical neglect of her hippie mother. I asked about her grandmother. She was a total control freak in a religious tradition that was strong on performance and weak on relationships.

Why did the daughter rebel? It was her own immature way of attempting to grow up. One of the sad parts of such adolescent rejection is that many of the values and parental guidelines were good. A student who gains his independence by force is called *rebellious* and rebellion is an unhealthy way to navigate into adulthood. There are many sad stories of students who literally went wild in college because they did not know how to manage their newfound independence.

When our youngest daughter turned 18, she commented that she could now vote and buy lottery tickets, cigarettes and porn magazines. Then she paused and said, "How sad it is that someone who is 18 is now legally free to destroy themselves financially, physically and morally."

THE MIND IS LOCKED SHUT

Teens that get extended lectures from strongly opinionated parents put a padlock on the door of their minds. They become very selective about what they hear and to whom they will listen.

There are three reasons adolescents mentally lock us out. One is when they are often subjected to lengthy lectures with little or no opportunity for feed-back. Family therapist, H. Norman Wright, in his book, *Pre-Hysteric Parenting*, warns that the greater the amount of verbiage that comes from us as parents, the more it closes a child's ears and mouth. Kids view the lecture as a long monologue (p.151).

The second reason is that parents often fail to practice what they preach. Kids rarely translate your wrong behavior into right behavior for themselves. Third, little effort is made to understand why the student has shut them out in the first place. Psychologist, Dr. Gary Oliver, reminds us that the last thing our children want is advice or criticism. They want to be understood. In the midst of their powerful emotions, they just want us to understand (Praise Kids, p. 288).

Take obnoxious behavior for example. When parents fail to give their teens healthy attention, it often results in obnoxious behavior. Author and counselor, Selwyn Hughes, suggests, "The child will begin to manifest extreme unacceptable behavior on the basis that attack is the best form of defense. This results in the child feeling the lesser pain of rejection for what he is. He finds it much easier to live with the knowledge that he is being rejected for his unacceptable behavior than with the knowledge that the rejection is due to his own worthlessness" (p. 69).

REBELLION

A mind closed toward God is usually very open to those who have no pretense of being religious. Their new identity now includes other rebels and cynics with similar disdain for their parents and other authority figures (Prov. 1:10-19).

This disdain for family that stems out of hurt and anger creates a void, an inner craving to belong. Think about the drug scene, gangs and cults. Christian youth will reject truth and swallow the lies of Satan if they feel accepted. Rebels all have at least one thing in common: they want to be independent! Their minds are inverted. To them rebellion is viewed as freedom.

The problem is that in their new "freedom" they get addicted to chemicals, gambling, money, food or relationships. The newly freed are then newly enslaved (2 Pet. 2:19).

LOVE/HATE RELATIONSHIPS

A child from an over-controlling home will live life on an emotional roller coaster. On one hand she may have developed an inordinate sense of dependence. Does she like being this way? No - she hates it! She may even hate you for making her an emotional cripple. On the other hand, she has a deep love and desire to be loved. How can this be? Simple, she will love you as her parent but hate you for what you did.

The dysfunction only deepens in adulthood as all contacts with the parents continue to be on a child-to-parent level rather than adult-to-adult. The emotion that keeps her locked in this love/hate relationship is an ongoing fear of rejection.

There are two challenging steps the adult child can take to begin to unlock this dysfunctional love/hate stalemate. First, is to forgive her parents for over-protecting. If it is not acknowledged and forgiven, it will be repeated in the adult child's family. Second, is to honestly identify and put away once and for all the childish behavioral patterns that have characterized her life (I Cor. 13:11). How? By acknowledging and renouncing childlike perceptions and behavioral patterns. These two brave steps can make a positive change in the adult child whether or not anything changes in her parents. In chapter 3 we will discuss how the love/hate effects of over-protection play out in a marriage.

EVER-PRESENT ANGER

The final pattern that stands head and shoulders above any other in the over-managed person is the constant presence of anger.

This anger may take many forms. First, as an *exploder*, she can be a rager, pan thrower, screamer or blow a fuse at the drop of a hat.

On the other hand, she may be an *imploder*. These are the passive-aggressive types. Often the expression of passive anger hurts the angry person more than the object of the anger. If grades are important to the parents, the student may just sabotage her grades. This inflames the parents but it also damages the student's education and future employment opportunities. It is all about revenge.

Finally, she can be a *runner* who escapes by turning to drugs, sex, sports, compulsions, hobbies, TV, computers, gangs, cars, money or books. The runner's greatest fear is that of confrontation and of experiencing potential rejection if she displays her anger openly. She needs you to make an effort to normalize the emotion of anger in the home by talking about emotions, both hers and yours.

Anger is expressed many ways but one common result is conflict. If you use the conflict to identify the needs and meet them in a healthy way, God's peace will begin to reign in your home.

We have surveyed some of the characteristics of over-protection you can recognize in the student's life. Next we will see what the legacy of over-protection looks like in the day-to-day life of an adult.

ANGER REDUCTION KEYS

1. Permit each child to make age-appropriate decisions.
2. Demonstrate unconditional love without behavioral conditions.
3. Be your child's cheerleader at each step towards adulthood.
4. Reduce your control at age-appropriate stages.
5. Look for any signs of low confidence in your child.
6. Ask God to give you the keys to unlock your child's mind if he has shut you out.
7. Understand why your child chooses the friends he does.
8. Identify your child's pattern of expressing anger and determine the need behind it.

SMALL GROUP DISCUSSION QUESTIONS

1. What personal experiences did you have with an over-controlling parent, guardian or mate? How did it make you feel? How did it affect you in life or in relationships?
2. How were you treated as a child? By whom? How did it feel? Why do you think they did it?
3. What are some positive ways your parents encouraged you to grow up? What are some ways you wish they had encouraged you?
4. In what ways did your parents increase your confidence in yourself and in God? How do you wish they would have done it?
5. How did you deal with rules and authority as you grew up? Why do you feel you responded that way? What effect did/does it have on you in adulthood?
6. How did your parents convey that they did or did not understand you? What was your response? How did/does it affect you in adulthood?
7. What kind of conflicts did you and your parents have over your friends? What was the basis of the conflicts? What were your parents' relationships to your friends? What do you wish they had done differently?
8. How was your anger dealt with by your parents? What effects did their response have on you? What have you learned from their responses to your anger?

CHAPTER 3

OVER-PROTECTION - AN ADULT LEGACY OF ANGER

IN CHAPTER 2 we discussed the stories of Brenda and Helen. Brenda is a young adult, raised all her life in Bible-believing churches. Helen is in her forties. She was raised in a nominally religious home quietly characterized by incest, adultery and alcohol. Both Brenda and Helen were raised by over-protective parents. The results of over-protection are the same whether it is a religious or nonreligious home. The reason for this is simple. Excessive control is usually fear-based and not faith-based. Whatever replaces genuine faith is usually characterized by sin (Rom. 14:23). There are eight characteristics that indicate fear-based parenting.

ADULT CHARACTERISTICS

INDECISION

Helen is racked with second-guessing herself. Yes, she is active in a small Bible study group that focuses on the thorough study and application of the Word of God. And yet her indecisive tendencies plague her. She struggles with a core belief that she cannot make the "right" decision in anything. As soon as a decision is made the "what ifs" pour into her thinking. "What if this does not look right?" "What if I get this wallpaper up and I hate it?"

She gets really upset at herself and, unfortunately, with everyone around her.

FEAR OF ABANDONMENT

Children are not the only ones who may have a fear of being alone. Adults, whether religious or not, can be subtly managed by the fear of abandonment. Controllers or over-protectors instill the lie into their spouses or children that they could not survive on their own - not just financially, but emotionally and psychologically.

Over-protectors insert themselves into every aspect of their child's or spouse's life. That unintentionally reinforces the lie that the spouse or child can't get along without them. Result? They marry strong, controlling mates who continue this dysfunction of inordinate dependency first learned in the home. Brenda told me that she literally believed her mom was God when she was growing up.

The greatest destruction an over-protective parent or spouse can inflict is to cause a person to factor God out of their emotional security system. The parent or spouse replaces God as his ultimate source of security. This lays the foundation for relational idolatry, popularly referred to as co-dependence. Because no human can perfectly meet the security needs of another, the fear of abandonment only increases.

FEAR OF FAILURE

The fear of failure is closely related to the fear of rejection. If you make a mistake or wrong decision or do not perform well, your failure could result in a significant person in your life devaluing you and throwing you back in disgust. That reflects the root meaning of the word rejection, "to throw back." Let's look at how this played out for Terri.

Terri's second home was the church. Her father was a church music director. Her mother micro-managed Terri. Every facet of her life was ordered by her mother. As Terri and I talked, I asked her to allow the Lord to bring the source of her fear of failure to her mind. It was not easy but she prayed with me that God would show her.

Terri began to recall that as a child her mother would get just as angry at her for a small childish infraction as she did for a major one. On a scale of 1-10, one being an insignificant infraction and ten being a major one, her over-critical mother reacted with the *same* intense anger for a level one infraction as she did a ten. Terri developed a fear of making even the smallest mistake.

This drove Terri straight into perfectionism. She became a black and white thinker. She felt she was either totally good or totally bad. She feared making the smallest mistake because she would have to face her mother's rejection. Result? Everything in Terri's life had to be perfect. If anything had a small flaw, it was totally bad. Worse yet, Terri would feel she was totally bad and deserved to be rejected. She always felt she was going to fall into total ruin; it was only a matter of *when,* not *if.* She became a substance abuser to numb that fear - the fear of failure and subsequent rejection. Oh, and yes, she is a believer.

CONSTANT AFFIRMATION

An adult who needs constant verbal affirmation or reassurance is emotionally stuck inside. After years of being constantly corrected by an over-protector, there is a constant need to know he is pleasing in every respect, all the time. They grow up craving reassurance.

The controlling adult instills within the spouse or child, the responsibility to please at all times or face being rejected. Please or perish! The recipient of this conditional acceptance is constantly in need of "that-a-boy" or "good girl." He will go to any lengths to please. He will also need to hear a verbal affirmation that he did indeed please and has not failed in his efforts.

One of the most common adult characteristics of this need for constant affirmation is seen in workaholics. "If I just work harder, I'll get more approval." Psychologist Dr. David Stoop believes that a workaholic is trying to cover his feelings of inadequacy with a thin veneer of accomplishment (p.112).

There are two common traits of a workaholic; first, an insatiable draw to public affirmation. It is not merely something that would be nice. *It is craved.* God calls it the praise of man (John 12:43). Workaholics look to gain satisfaction from man instead of God.

The second trait of the workaholic is the desire to escape from failing or potentially failing in a relationship at home. Workaholics seeking approval rarely have good relationships at home. Work becomes an "acceptable" excuse to get praise on one hand and avoid a difficult situation at home on the other.

NEED TO CONTROL

A need to be in control at all times does not reflect spiritual maturity. Why? The root of this need for excessive control goes back to fear, not faith. Dads are pointedly commanded not to exasperate their children (Col. 3:21). Major sources of exasperation are over-protection and excessive control.

Pastors are cautioned by God not to lord it over those they are responsible for (I Peter 5:3). The words "lording it over" convey the idea of domineering, as in the practice of a strong person dominating one who is weak. God's sheep are to be *led*, not driven (John 10:3-4). Whenever adults are failing to lead by example they will usually resort to the use of anger for harsh domination and control. This kind of leadership is characterized by anger, manipulation and fear. Its fruit is inevitable - anger in the home, at work and in the church.

Marriage can be a perfect setup for power perversion. If there ever was a misused teaching from Scripture, it is that of submission. It is a biblical concept (Eph. 5:22-33) but any truth taken out of balance results in abuse. This concept has been used as a whip to control a spouse not because it is morally right, but out of fear of not being in control. Any spouse who uses power to control the other *outwardly* is basically struggling with fear and anxiety *inwardly*. A mate who seeks to dominate and control the other through finances, sex, relationships, home management or major decision making no doubt was hurt as a kid by some-one. Now the hurt continues in adulthood to the embitterment of all. Without a doubt, the number one emotion a controlling person uses is anger.

Still a Kid

Having fun and a free-spirited sense of humor is healthy in adulthood. Playing with the kids or your spouse is wholesome fun. That is not what is meant by the phrase, "He's still a kid." It refers to an adult who is stuck emotionally as a kid. He still relates as a child does to an adult, especially toward parents or other authority figures.

In the book, *You Can Work It Out*, I shared the full story of Traci, a woman who after her marriage, still related to her divorced mother on a child-to-parent basis instead of adult-to-adult. Her phone conversations with her mother sounded like those of a young adolescent talking to a strict parent. Traci would punctuate every other sentence with, "Sorry."

An over-protective parent forces the child to remain in a child's role regardless of age. One of the most difficult tasks an over-parented adult child undertakes is that of making a mental shift from a child perspective to an adult perspective.

Every adult needs to relate to his parents adult-to-adult out of honor. Honor is not obedience to parents' wishes or commands. It is a deep respect that can say, "No," in love, when appropriate. What is the alternative? Adults who cannot say "No" when appropriate develop a deep sense of bitterness for saying, "Yes." Responsible adults can say, "No thank you" honorably with conviction. The emotionally stuck adult must follow the Apostle Paul's example to grow up and put away the childish perspectives and practices (I Cor. 13:11).

RELATIONSHIP ADDICTION

You may be familiar with the term "codependent". Drs. Minirth and Meier define it as an addiction to people, behaviors or things (*Love is a Choice*, p. 11). It was originally used in the alcohol recovery literature to describe a wife who was dependent on the relationship with her alcoholic husband and the husband was dependent on the alcohol, thus the term co-dependent (Friel, *Adult Children*, p. 155). Later the word was used to describe people, regardless of gender, who were overly dependent on each other.

The codependent person, raised to be dependent by over-protection, unconsciously makes another human act like his God-substitute in at least four areas:

- Omnipotence - God is all powerful. This human substitute is expected to be able to fix, deal with and protect the person from everything. Failure to do so will incur the dependent one's wrath.

- Omnipresent - God is all present. His human replacement must always be there for the person whether it is humanly possible or not. He panics if the God-substitute is not there or within reach at a moment's notice.
- Omniscience - God is all knowing. The human replacement is expected to always know what we think and anticipate our every move and react accordingly. You will hear in a codependent argument the accusation; "You should have known I needed that!"
- Immutability - God's character never changes. The person elevated to the place of God must be predictable, even-keeled, without mood swings, always accepting, absolutely stable like a rock. Change is not welcome; it threatens the other person's comfort zones which are defined by fear.

Codependence is displeasing to the Lord! Jesus plainly stated, "He who loves (is dependent upon) father and mother more than Me is not worthy of Me: and he who loves (depends upon) son or daughter more than Me is not worthy of Me" (Matt. 10:37). Why? Psychologist, Dr. Robert Hemfelt and behavioral pediatrician, Dr. Paul Warren, in their book, *Kids Who Carry Our Pain,* make it very clear. "In a codependent family the members are either walking around with an emptiness inside them or are carrying the pain of this emptiness for someone else in the family" (p. 14). Who do they turn to in order to fill the empty hole in their soul? Not God, but people. They substitute people in place of God for their needs.

The following list is a summary of the general characteristics of believers who are relationship addicted or codependent. They have not navigated successfully out of childhood, emotionally or spiritually.

1. They are clueless as to what "normal" is. Their birth family, with all of its control, is viewed as normal.
2. They find it difficult to follow through with a project. Such people tend to be impulsive and easily distracted.
3. They judge themselves without mercy. As a result they have a low appreciation of themselves, their talents or God's gifts in their lives.
4. Any change causes an overreaction. Change totally threatens their security.
5. The need for constant approval or affirmation drives them. They have little idea who they really are in terms of identity because of their extreme desire to please. They never did their "identity" homework.
6. There is a lack of confidence in making decisions. There is little sense of being led by God's Spirit.
7. They have an inability to see alternatives to situations, thus they relate very impulsively. They are classic black and white thinkers. They just cannot see choices other than the extremes.
8. Dependent people live in fear of abandonment. God's eternal presence is replaced by the need for someone else's human presence.
9. They are confused about love, pity, boundaries and their own circle of responsibility. Tough or responsible love is virtually foreign to them.
10. They are very rigid with a need to control or be controlled. They are inflexible and must be in control to avoid facing any change.

The New York Times bestseller, *Codependent No More* by Melody Beattie, contains exhaustive lists of codependent characteristics under such headings as caretaking, low self-worth, repression, obsession, controlling, denial, dependency, poor communication, weak boundaries, lack of trust, sex problems and anger. A tremendous amount of anger is the result when the "God-substitute" fails to perform to the codependent's expectations and assigned roles.

ROLES ARE REVERSED

An adult who is stuck emotionally as a kid triggers a great deal of anger in a child through emotional incest. Physical incest is using a child to meet adult sexual needs. Emotional incest is an adult using a child to meet the adult's emotional needs.

Children are treated like "little spouses." The adult leans on the child for the emotional support that should be coming from another adult. By sharing his inner struggles, marital problems and even sexual conflicts, the parent makes the child his counselor instead of getting appropriate help from a friend, pastor or Christian counselor.

In such cases, children are asked to meet emotional needs in their parents that the adults can't even meet on their own peer level! Sadly, the parents are asking *from* their child what they should be providing *for* their child. The roles are reversed.

What is the net effect of this role reversal? Ultimately it robs children of their childhood, increases dependence and cripples their emotional growth. This results in deep seated anger and long term bitterness in the birth family and in the adult child's own marriage. No child or adult child wants to feel obligated to meet the parent's emotional security needs that should be met by the spouse and ultimately by God (Psalm 73:25).

The Old Testament priest, Eli, apparently needed approval from his two wicked sons, Hophni and Phinehas, and feared their rejection (1 Sam. 1:3; 2:12-13). He refused to correct their immoral behavior and failed to act responsibly toward his adult sons. His irresponsible behavior resulted in a series of events that ultimately cost Eli and his two sons their lives (I Sam. 2:22, 29).

ADULT REASONS FOR OVER-PROTECTION

We have described eight characteristics of an adult who was over-protected and over-controlled as a child. Now we want to answer the hard question: What are four reasons adults attempt to control each other and their children by over-protection?

FEAR OF RE-EXPERIENCING EMOTIONAL PAIN

Joyce always went to church with her mom. Her dad went infrequently. Her parents fought a lot. Mom made every attempt to make up to Joyce for what her father failed to do. Dad was self-employed. His small engine repair shop brought them a modest income but it did take most of his time and energy. If he was not working, he filled the role of the proverbial couch potato. Television was like his drug of choice to avoid interaction with his wife.

This avoidance strategy was also played out on Joyce. Dad was there but not there. He did not show any interest in her private music lessons or school activities. The emotional scars were deep in Joyce. Emotional abandonment is every bit as painful as physical abandonment.

Joyce determined that when she married and became a mother, her kids would never suffer by her absence. She chose to inject herself in every aspect of their lives. Unintentionally she made them feel they could not function in life without her. In fact, they were expected to think her thoughts, hold her views, maintain her standards and embody her passion for politics. They were never going to feel what she had felt as a child.

Joyce was always angry about something. If her children did not respond as she programmed them to, she went ballistic. Why? She feared her kids might experience the hurtful things she had experienced if they did not conform to her attempts to protect them. But why the anger? Because their age appropriate behavior threatened her goal of control. Joyce could not figure out why her children would not cooperate with her in preventing a recurrence of what she experienced as a child. There was a good reason they didn't. They never knew what her childhood was like or what she was trying to protect them from. She was going to both fix and avoid reliving her past.

Joyce failed to understand two things. First, she was different from her mother. Second, she had a good scriptural foundation her mother did not have. Had she acted on those two facts alone, her children would never have had to be the objects of their mother's fear-based control. She would not re-experience old emotional pain.

However, Joyce had virtually factored God out of her relationships. She could not trust God with her worries. Joyce knew He would let trials into her life that she would not want (James 1:2-4). Joyce's desire to live a pain-free life only energized her fear. Her fear came out in anger which erupted with volcanic proportions when her kids did not fulfill that pain-free assignment.

Any adult who is still controlled in the present by past emotional hurts would benefit by considering these questions:

1. Are there past *issues* that you avoid at all costs? Remember, the past that is not processed is always present. Avoidance

is a form of denial. Denial is preventing God access to a hurt that He wants to heal for your benefit and His glory.

2. Are there certain *emotions* that are being blocked because they will trigger other past hurtful emotions?

3. Are there certain geographical *locations* you avoid or *celebrations* that are not emotionally safe to revisit?

4. Are there certain *events* that are being blocked from your mind? For example: occasions of past rejection, abandonment, failure, loneliness, financial loss, poverty, memories of not being loved or feeling unlovable.

There is at least one good reason to uncover those sources and process them biblically. Failure to do so may cause you to obsess on your spouse's or child's behavior to avoid re-feeling past emotional pain. If you are totally focused on your kids or spouse, you may be attempting to avoid dealing with the ghosts of your past. A focus on other people's "stuff" helps you to avoid your own "stuff."

No child or adult can ever successfully shield you from re-feeling your past pain. All the anger in the world will not guarantee you emotional protection. There's one reason it won't. It is not God's will to protect your past but to work through it biblically. Obsessing on a child or spouse is a poor substitute for God's healing in your life.

FEAR OF PARENTAL FAILURE

Over-protection can be rooted in the subconscious need to avoid re-feeling past pain. It can also be rooted in the fear of failure of being a good parent.

Brad and Joyce initially came for marriage counseling. As we began to identify their other issues, I heard Joyce state off-handedly that she did not want to fail as a parent. It soon became clear Joyce was also managed by the fear of failure.

Fear transformed Joyce into a classic micro-manager. Every word, thought, action or attitude expressed by her children was meticulously scrutinized for a flaw in her parenting. She tenaciously screened their comportment to see if she was failing in any way, shape or form. She was totally focused on herself. Every action of her children was a litmus test of her parenting skills.

Tempers flared if Joyce's husband would not support her schemes and strategies designed to validate her as a parent. Joyce bought into the lie that her personal value was basically tied to her children's behavior. God never gave children the responsibility to preserve their parents' worth. That must be totally based on our relationship with Jesus Christ (Gal. 2:20). Although each of us as parents and grandparents have made our share of mistakes, those shortcomings do not change our value in Christ. That remains a gift from God, not an earned reward for quality parenting (Eph. 2:8-9).

Our kids will learn more from our corrected failures than from our untarnished successes or hidden failures. Tragically, children who grow up with "perfect parents" sense early in life that they cannot measure up to their parents' standards and gradually stop trying. They become passive-aggressive in their expression of anger. This only infuriates the parents more and greatly limits the God-designed potential of the youth. Anger comes, peace goes.

Fear They will be Like Me

The next root of control is also related to failure. This fear goes deeper. It is the fear that our children will turn out like us. Alton knew this fear well.

Alton was a former drug addict. His youth was character-ized by drugs, alcohol, rebellion, gangs, immorality and crime. Not exactly an average American youth. His dad abandoned the family early in his life and his mom had to work two jobs to make ends meet. As a result, he was raised on the streets in a small California community. Actually, the neighborhood raised him.

Years later he encountered the claims of Christ, became a believer and experienced unconditional love in a Christian drug rehab center. It was while at the rehab center he met and mar-ried his wife. She already had one child from a former marriage. Soon they had two of their own. Guess what kind of parenting style he adopted? Right! Over-protection.

Alton had a lot of baggage from his past, including guilt, shame, fear, loss and regret. He unconsciously said to himself, *"No kid of mine will ever go through what I went through."* Now, how did he parent? Just like Joyce did, but instead of fearing he would fail as a parent, he scrutinized his kids for any potential symptoms that they were heading down his old road. He would rather die than see that happen. He made his rebellious past his standard to avoid instead of making his present goal of Christ-likeness his standard to achieve. His focus should have been on how he could influence his kids to be like the Lord Jesus Christ *now*.

What could Alton do differently? Simply evaluate anything that he or his parents did. If it was *like* Christ, *keep* it, reproduce it. If it was *not* like Christ, reject it. This completely shifts the focus from what the children should not do to what they can do to become more like Jesus. This positive focus would greatly reduce the fear of seeing his negative traits reproduced in his children.

FEAR OF NOT BEING LOVED

Pauline wanted to get pregnant. She did not care how. She was willing to give sex to any guy. She was not promiscuous because she wanted sex. It was for an emotional reason; she wanted to be loved. Pauline reasoned that if she had a child she would raise it in such a way that it would love her unconditionally all the rest of her life. The child's assignment was to lavish love on Mom. There was one small problem with that strategy. Children start to walk away from us into independence almost from the day they are born.

Pauline was a very fearful and angry mom. She made her daughter's every action a test of her love for her mom. Most every request was preceded with; "If you love me" or "You wouldn't do that if you loved me." The fear of not loving Mommy enough totally controlled her daughter. It was all or nothing. Either she totally loved Mom by being compliant, obedient, perfect, affirming, loving and physically affectionate or she did not love her at all. Even normal childlike behavior was met by "You don't love me" statements.

No human can ultimately fill the hole in your soul as a result of not feeling loved. Only one person can. Jesus explained this to the woman at the well who was also trying to fill the void in her life through men, "Whoever drinks of the water that I will give him shall never thirst: but the water that I will give him will become in him a well of water springing up to eternal life" (Jn. 4:14). The water Jesus referred to was an inner well-spring which is a word picture of the Holy Spirit (Jn. 7:38-39). The first fruit that reveals the presence of the Holy Spirit is love (Gal. 5:22-23).

Anything or anybody you use as a "God-substitute" will fail you and anger will be a normal response notifying you of that failure. God has gone on record to affirm incredible love for you

(Rom. 8:5). As you understand this in the depth of your soul, you can deal with any human rejection. It will still hurt but it will not devastate you, leaving you debilitated emotionally.

Roots of over-protection can come into your life from many sources. We have only surveyed four of them:

1. Fear of re-experiencing emotional pain
2. Fear of parental failure
3. Fear that the kids will turn out like us
4. Fear of not being loved

It may be hard to believe that someone can struggle with these issues and still be a Christian. But to quote André Crouch, "If I never had a problem, I wouldn't know that He could solve them. I would not know what faith in God could do."

We have looked at over-protection from a child's perspective and surveyed the results of these characteristics in adults. Now it's time to gain a bigger picture of anger and over-control from God's perspective. We have hinted at it all along. God condenses the issue down to one short verse that is a key to promoting peace in any relationship.

ANGER REDUCTION KEYS

1. Replace fear with faith in managing your family.
2. Affirm your value as a parent in your relationship with Jesus Christ and not in your children's performance.
3. Honestly face any symptoms of being a workaholic and make the necessary corrections.
4. Release your family from the ultimate responsibility to make you happy.
5. Identify and put away any childish ways carried over from your childhood.
6. Choose to relate with your adult children and parents, adult-to-adult.
7. Biblically work through any past hurts that still seem to manage you in adulthood.

SMALL GROUP DISCUSSION QUESTIONS

1. Consider the eight characteristics of an adult who has been over-protected or controlled as a youth. What has been your experience with them personally or as you observed them in someone else?
2. How has this over-protection affected your family or someone else's?
3. How would you attempt to explain the reality that sincere believers struggle in these areas?
4. What are some of the appropriate or inappropriate methods you have seen in yourself or others to correct them?
5. Describe how you feel the over-protected one views God. How would you explain why they have this particular view of God?
6. Of the four primary sources of fear that result in over-protection, which ones have you seen the most and in whom did you see them? How did they influence you personally?
7. How would you answer the four questions regarding past emotional hurt on page 11? What steps have you taken or would suggest to another to take to correct them? Have you seen them work effectively?
8. What additional characteristics have you seen in adults that may indicate they were over-controlled or over-protected? Were you able to help them? How did you do it? Over the long haul, what was the result?

CHAPTER 4

OVER-PROTECTION, GOD'S PERSPECTIVE

I WAS SITTING in Alton's living room enjoying an evening of fellowship. Suddenly he catapulted out of his chair and darted into his son's bedroom. "What is going on in here?" he demanded in a gruff voice. "I know you are doing something!" After reassuring him they were just playing, he left with a threat that he'd better not need to come back. Later my daughter who was playing in the room asked me what that was all about. "Beats me," I shrugged.

At dinner Alton obsessed on every bite his thirteen-year-old son ate, totally ignoring any of his younger daughter's behavior. His son did not talk right. He did not walk right. He did not dress right. Nothing was right. Over the years Alton's son shut down emotionally. He was a textbook adolescent living with a very controlling, critical dad. To look at Alton's son, one word said it all: *exasperated.*

EXASPERATION IS A SIN

Most parents are familiar with the verse, "Children, obey your parents in the Lord, for this is right" (Eph. 6:1). For every relational truth in scripture there is a counter balancing truth. The balancing truth to children obeying their parents is brief. It's simple. It contains no big words. "Fathers, do not exasperate your children so that they will not lose heart" (Col. 3:20). The

Amplified translation renders it "Fathers, don't scold your children so much that they become discouraged and quit trying."

The words *"provoke"* or *"exasperate"* basically mean *"to irritate, agitate"* or, to put it simply, *"to nag at habitually."* Welcome to over-control, over-parenting and over-protection. This sinful parenting pattern, whether done by a dad or mom, has three characteristics: demanding commands, perpetual fault-finding and interference for interference sake.

DEMANDING COMMANDS

I never served in the military but many of my friends who proudly served would tell me about their boot camp experiences. One thing was perfectly clear. When a D. I. (Drill Instructor) told them to do something, they did it. Pleasantries were skipped. Orders were short and not sweet! Every order was a demanding command. They had the power, authority, right and responsibility to demand instant obedience. Failure to respond to a command was dealt with severely. There is a place for a command to be issued and instantly obeyed. It's in the military, not in the home.

Demanding commands, whether issued by a mom or dad, are not good. Harshness, irritation or frustration sends a message that children are not valued. If they do not feel valued by you they will not value themselves. The result will be anger with you for devaluing them and they may also direct their anger toward themselves resulting in depression or other negative emotions.

Parents who issue demanding commands rarely know what *gentle* respect is. Authoritarian control is their goal with little sensitivity to feelings. There is a reason for it. Authoritarian behaviors are not done for the benefit of the person being controlled. They are primarily for the emotional benefit of the fear-based controlling parent.

What's the alternative? Issue appropriate, respectful and firm requests. Then add the most popular word in the English language that conveys respect, "Please."

When our girls were younger, we would emphasize the importance of saying, "Please" when making a request. DeeDee once asked if I would pass the spaghetti. I gently asked, "What is the magic word?" Then I heard the forced response, "Please." Good. We passed the spaghetti. A few minutes later I made the same request omitting the magic word. From the mouth of a four-year-old came a respectful request, "What's the magic word?" I sat there, nodded my head, then broke into a smile and said, "Please." I could have firmly told her it is not her responsibility to correct her father but that would have shut her down emotionally. That is usually the response of an immature parent who feels threatened.

Perpetual Fault-Finding

I like Fred. His life has given me much writing material. Often he drops by my office and insists on taking me out to lunch. When we get into his car I hear all kinds of noise coming from a small box on the dashboard. It screeches and squeals. It is a radar detector and its primary purpose is to warn the driver that there is a police officer ahead with a radar detector which objectively tells the officer exactly how fast the oncoming car is traveling.

Civilians have radar detectors to warn them of an officer ahead checking the driver's speed. I have often thought, "Why not just set one's cruise control at the appropriate speed and relax?" Sorry. People with radar detectors wish to exceed the posted speed limits without getting caught.

Over-protective, controlling parents or spouses use their mental "radar guns" constantly to check the behavioral "speed" of all the members of the family. They are constantly on the lookout for any flaws, mistakes or signs of disrespect. As soon as one is detected, it is brought to the attention of the offender.

Yes, parents need to monitor behavior in the home, but positive behavior does not draw the attention of the controlling parent. Only flaws, mistakes or instances of failing to measure up to some idealistic standard will catch the notice of the controlling parent's "radar."

We had a pastor friend and his wife over for dinner and they brought their teenage daughter with them. She was a delightful person. Her mother, an unrecovered critic, corrected her sixteen-year-old daughter throughout the meal. I lost count at twenty times. Despite my efforts to change the subject, I could not get her to stop reviewing all her daughter's flaws in our presence. Why did she do that?

The over-controlling parent is primarily motivated by fear, especially rejection. What was her mother's fear? She feared that we would see an unnoticed and uncorrected flaw in her daughter and think she was a bad mother. The perpetual fault finder cannot let up. The object of their criticism can rarely relax. The hyper-critic can foster obsessive/compulsive behavior and set up a child or adolescent for such trauma as panic attacks and eating disorders in both adolescence and adulthood.

Perpetual fault-finding is the second pattern of parenting that offends God and can create a bottomless reservoir of anger in our children and spouse. The third source of exasperation is interference just for the sake of interference.

UNNECESSARY INTERFERENCE

Recall my visit to Alton's home. Our kids were playing nicely in his daughter's bedroom when he bolted for her room to see what was going on. My wife, Linda, and I exchanged glances, wondering if we had missed something.

During the visit we repeatedly observed Alton's checking on his kids and quizzing them on what they were doing. He even interfered with his wife's dinner preparation with unsolicited suggestions. He stuck his proverbial nose in things whenever he felt like it.

Often when a young person is working through a problem the best way he knows how, an intrusive adult will insist on getting involved. That results in the youth getting angry and sometimes giving up. He thinks, "What's the use?" The motive behind the overly intrusive adult is another fear-based way to control and be in control. Information is power.

The topic of intrusiveness is one of the bases of the bestseller book, *Boundaries*, by Dr. Henry Cloud and Dr. John Townsend. Personal boundary violations among believers are so prevalent that it made *Boundaries* a bestseller. Why? It addressed how to correct a major dysfunctional pattern of behavior that is just as identifiable in the church as anywhere else.

The book *Boundaries* focuses primarily on personal boundary issues from the outside in. Our book, *You Can Work It Out*, focuses on our circles of responsibilities from the inside out. It describes how to identify, assign, assume and fulfill what is in your own circle of responsibility or boundary.

Nothing exasperates a child, youth or adult more than for another person to interfere intrusively and unnecessarily into his or her life whether it is work, play, study or service. Let's take a look at how God views the unhealthy process of exasperating children.

A COMMAND, NOT ADVICE

In the Greek New Testament there are at least two ways to express a desire for someone to do something. The first is a strong urging or pleading, for example, "Therefore I urge you, brethren, by the mercies of God, to present your bodies a living and holy sacrifice, acceptable to God, which is your spiritual service of worship" (Romans 12:1).

The second way is to make a direct command. The Apostle Paul used a direct command when he wrote, "Fathers, do not exasperate your children." (Col. 3:21). This is a command of God to be obeyed in no uncertain terms. Because it is a present tense command, it can be translated, "Do not keep on provoking (nagging, exasperating) your children." He is commanding fathers to end this commonly practiced behavior. The apostle describes the mental, emotional and spiritual damage this cruel form of parenting inflicts. There are four negative results when people exasperate one another. The first consequence is that it damages lives.

Damages Lives

What happens when Christian parents provoke or exasperate their family members to anger? A word picture would be helpful here. In World War II, many American prisoners of war experienced cruel forms of torture. Some of it was done to satisfy the sadistic tendencies of their captors. Much of it was designed to break the will to resist their captors. It was also an effective barbaric means of extracting classified information.

One form of torture was Chinese water torture. A POW would be tied down on his back with his arms outstretched in the hot sun with no food to eat or water to drink. A can of water was suspended above his head with a small hole in it to allow a drop of water to drip down at regular intervals. Initially it was a nuisance, an irritant. Soon each succeeding drop developed into an excruciating, painful thud that felt like the head would split open anytime. This form of torture broke even the most determined soldier. Many broke down emotionally or just went insane.

Just like water torture, perpetual fault-finding, interference and demanding commands provoke negative behavior. God describes the effect if this pattern is not corrected, "Fathers [and mothers], do not exasperate your children, that they may not lose heart," or that they may become discouraged, lose hope and quit trying.

When your spouse, child or teen "*loses heart*" or hope because of demanding commands, perpetual fault-finding and unnecessary interference, it could damage their emotions.

DAMAGES EMOTIONS

In his book, *The Key to Your Child's Heart*, Dr. Gary Smalley points out that a broken or closed spirit can result from damaged emotions. A closed spirit is characterized by withdrawing, shutting down or just checking out (p. 20). You can see this lack of responsiveness in those who have shut down inside. In extreme cases, there is a total lack of emotional response. Why? If they have to connect with people at any level, they run the risk of getting hurt again. No connection means no pain. They will work, come home, eat and veg out in front of the TV, computer or cell phone and go to bed. There is very little interaction with the spouse or kids. They are present but not there emotionally.

DISTORTS THE CONSCIENCE

To be emotionally shut down does not mean there is no conscience. Instead one may have an overactive conscience that leads to constant self-blame and guilt. Sometimes this is observable in a person who punctuates each paragraph with the word, "Sorry."

An over-sensitive conscience can lead to the feeling that everything is your fault regardless of how incidental. The self-condemnation is a natural outgrowth of a history of being constantly criticized. She tends to view things that happen to her as a natural consequence of being bad, broken, defective, and of little value. It reflects self-rejection. In a relationship she becomes a "doormat." Religiously, she is found regularly at the altar of the church, pouring out all the past week's guilt for failing to measure up, satisfy, be perfect and please everyone.

DEPRESSES THE WILL

What does "losing heart" do to the will? The will ceases to function normally. The power of choice is gone. "I can" is replaced with, "I can't." "I can't" is replaced with, "I won't try." One step more takes, "I can do all things through Christ" (Phil. 4:13) which becomes, "I don't dare try anything for Christ. To try is to come face to face with the possibility of more failure, criticism and ultimately rejection and hopelessness."

Provoking others to anger and discouragement takes its toll in damaged emotions, a distorted (condemning) conscience and a depressed will. The primary emotion coming from one who was hurt is anger. Anger becomes a defense mechanism. It now spills out on anyone around; at home, school, work or on the road. But there *is* an alternative.

ENCOURAGE AGE-APPROPRIATE CHOICES

If there is one statement I hear most from parents who have troubled teens it is this, "They are making bad choices." Or another variation of this, "We are really upset about the choices they are making." With only rare exception, after gaining some family history from *both* the parents and teens, one common picture emerges. Adolescents who make poor choices usually were not gradually trained to make wise choices. They were only told what to do.

Poor choices in adulthood often have their roots in childhood. Giving children age-appropriate choices early in life is therefore very important. Take clothes for example. Most parents dress their young children for the benefit of other adults and not for the sake of the kids. A mismatched outfit chosen by a child would be a mortifying experience for the mother at church. One creative option is to give the child a choice of two or three outfits that have been previously selected. Teach them early to make choices. Every time our young daughters asked us what they were to wear, we would ask them what their options were first.

While in the toy section of a large department store we gave our four-year-old permission to pick out a toy. To my pleasant surprise she responded, "What are my options?" She learned early that life is a matter of choices. The earlier they learn the better.

Life confronts us daily with choices. If we always tell children what to do and think, how will they learn to make good choices? Only a naive parent thinks he can tell his children what to do all through their developmental years and expect them to know how to make healthy decisions in adulthood.

Life is full of opportunities to choose early. Friends, food, hobbies, appropriate videos, TV programs and spending money are just a few. Due to busy schedules or even laziness, parents do not spend time teaching children or adolescents how to make appropriate decisions. Controlling parents convey that they know the best choice in every situation. This may be true but how did they learn to do so?

DISTINGUISH BETWEEN MORALS AND TASTE

More parent and teen arguments over clothes revolve around personal taste and parental pride rather than a moral issue. While shopping with our youngest daughter, Michelle, when she was in middle school, I took one look at a sweatshirt she was trying on and remarked, "You have that thing inside out." She retorted, "Oh, Dad, this is the style today." I could have given her lecture 47-C, (C for Chuck), that it was wrong inside out and looked ridiculous. I bit the bullet and said, "Interesting." She bought and wore it inside out. Was this a moral issue? No. Was it a preteen taste issue? Yes!

One of the reasons I enjoyed shopping with our girls was to have an opportunity to discuss appropriate clothes. Occasionally I was even invited to go shopping with our college daughter. I cannot remember the last time I asked her if she thought something was too tight, revealing or inappropriate. She points this out to me now, but over the years literally scores of hours at the mall were invested to produce this outcome.

When Michelle came home with a new pair of elevator shoes purchased with her own Christmas money, I thought to myself, "These shoes are not a moral issue but a taste issue and for her it is a good choice because it was *her* choice." But when Michelle sees me ready to go out the door in my mid-life attire and exclaims, "Dad, you're not wearing *that* are you?" I think, "What happened to my taste?" Now the issue switches from my taste to her preference. I change clothes! Take hope. They will grow out of these stages but constant controlling only prolongs the process.

LEARN FROM WRONG CHOICES

It is a fact of life that everyone, including our children, will make wrong choices. Let your children learn from wrong choices as early and cheaply as possible before the consequences become worse.

Michelle loves overnight parties with her church friends but when she loses a lot of sleep she is susceptible to a sore throat. So when she asked if she could attend an overnight event, I wanted to say no. I knew she would get sick the next day and pay for it for days. I asked her if she felt she might get sick if she went. She brushed it off. I told her it was her decision. She went and was sick for two days. Would you like to guess how many overnights she asked to attend the rest of her high school career? None. She now stays until midnight, has a blast and comes home. Why? Because she chooses to do so. She understands her own physical limits.

When a friend's son got busted for drugs I responded, "What a learning activity!" I urged the dad not to bail him out and let the courts teach him the reality of cause and effect. The court kept his case on hold for a year and a half. He did not know for all that time what the final outcome was going to be. He knew one thing. He'd better stay clean. God used that situation in his life to protect him during a difficult time. He is out of school now and working full-time.

Learning experiences can be expensive. Over-protective parents who repeatedly "bail out" their children will accomplish a short-range goal of saving the family pride and their child's pain but ultimate failure is almost assured in the future. Let them feel the pain of wrong choices early. It is their best insurance against major failures later. If you can't do this you may need to examine why you must have control.

AVOID THE USE OF SHAME

Shame, next to anger, is a major tool of control, manipulation and over-protection. While criticism attacks a person's actions, shame attacks the person's identity. It is one thing to help a person see the error of their wrong choice but it is quite another to shame them for it. Words like stupid, brainless, dummy or idiot all attack the core of a person. Comments such as, "Can't you do anything right?" "Here, I'll do it for you. You'll never get it right." "If I want it done right I'll just have to do it myself" and "If you had the brain of a duck you'd fly backwards" are all shaming statements. Such shaming words have even come out of Christian homes. These words steeped in shame trigger painful memories of what was said to them as kids by critical adults.

No twelve-year-old is going to reflect the mature decision making process of a forty-year-old parent. Your failure to make allowances for immaturity and time to grow is not the child's problem. It's your problem.

When you allow a person to make appropriate decisions and choices you are reflecting the ways of God. Adam and Eve were given a choice in the garden even when God knew full well they would suffer the consequences of their decision (Gen. 2:16-17). The power of choice is both a right and a responsibility God gives you. What you do with it will ultimately determine both your quality of life on earth and your eternal destiny.

ENCOURAGE THE EXPRESSION OF OPINIONS

Allowing family members to make choices is important. Equally important is allowing them to express their opinion appropriately and respecting them for it. Controllers do not value others' opinions. You see this personified in a totalitarian government. The whole motivation behind the suppression of independent ideas and thoughts is to maintain power and control. It is totally fear-based, not faith-based.

In a legalistic family system the parent's opinion is the only opinion. It is their way or the highway. Opinionated believers are insecure, immature and arrogant. Being opinionated is a form of control based on fear, whether expressed at home or at church. Truth can always stand investigation. Opinions cannot.

Another reason you may be afraid of another's opinion is the fear that you might have to accept it if you acknowledge it. If you do accept the other's opinion you may feel you have lost some preconceived notion of control. Often family fights are over getting someone to recognize or acknowledge the other person's position. A sign of maturity is the ability to acknowledge another's view without feeling your own position or security is threatened.

Over-controlling parents don't want to know their children's opinions and rarely have a clue what their kids are actually thinking. If they did they would be shocked! Not allowing them to express their opinions unknowingly trains children to lie to parents and themselves about their true feelings.

Husbands and wives can also lie about their true feelings. This blocks intimacy and furthers isolation. Being dishonest about feelings can come from having been shamed, criticized, interrupted, belittled or cut off when attempts were made to express them in the past. When this happens to students they are not able to discuss what's important to them or benefit from appropriate open discussion.

Adults need to remember that their current belief system had to be hammered out on the anvil of life through many detours, dead ends and rabbit trails. Forming a life belief system takes time and growth. Failure to allow that growth process results in what I observed to be the number one reason Christian students lost their faith in college. They had no galvanized faith of their own. In reality they lost their parent's faith, not theirs. They were never provided a safe environment to process their thoughts into their own mature convictions.

If a student is not free to explore his doubts, thoughts and questions with his parents, the likelihood is that this part of his development will remain stunted. He will not know what he believes or why he believes it. He will depend on someone else's belief system. This makes him an easy target for false religions that prey on personal acceptance as a way of disarming the uninformed. When a young person finds his beliefs challenged, he is not able to give a reason for the hope that is in him (I Pet. 3:15).

Allowing even the most cherished beliefs to be discussed and challenged is important. The Bereans were honored by the Apostle Paul because they did not blindly accept what he preached (Acts 17:10-11). They searched the Old Testament scriptures to see if what he was saying was true. Paul knew that truth would stand the test of scrutiny. Truth will vindicate itself.

The micro-managing parent who is fearful of losing control does not allow the child to explore his thoughts openly or express his opinions. Open discussion of ideas is the child's way to mature his ideas. It is therefore important not to shame any family member as he expresses his opinion. If he is shamed he will ask you to get off his train of growth and will go at it alone. Sadly both lose when that happens.

Children by nature are self-centered but as they are given the freedom to explore their thoughts with you, your acceptance and appropriate input will allow them to grow into balanced inter-dependence. Your failure to let this happen will result in an emotionally crippled, dependent person who will harbor a great deal of anger and resentment throughout his adult life.

Is there room within the family of Christ for differences of opinion? Just a surface reading of Romans 14 brings you to a solid *yes*. In this chapter Paul describes how one person values one day above another and yet another believer views every day alike. What is the Apostle's conclusion? "Each person must be fully convinced in his *own* mind" (Rom. 14:5). Such liberty would drive a control freak crazy. Since controllers are usually black and white thinkers it has to be either one way or another.

Acknowledging another's opinion does not necessarily imply acceptance. It is not a sin to acknowledge an opinion different from yours but it is a sign of respect to at least give them the benefit of their opinion and allow time and maturity to develop their perspective. Discipleship is learning and learning takes time.

PERMIT NORMAL EMOTIONS

Anger is the most lied about emotion among believers. "I'm not angry, I'm just frustrated." Frustration is the believer's euphemism for anger.

It would seem logical to some that upon conversion to Christianity all negative emotions should have been eliminated. Unfortunately that is not the case. The only emotion that is publicly allowed and encouraged in the church is joy. Believers can't be sad, fearful, angry, jealous or envious. God forbid that they ever get depressed. Just as none of our normal biological functions ceased at conversion, neither did any of our normal emotional expressions.

Controllers insist on having their children or mates limit their expression of emotions. There is a dysfunctional reason for it. Controllers do not know how to respond to the normal range of emotions in a healthy way themselves. Emotions scare them. The ability to control a person is in direct proportion to the ability to control someone's emotions. Remember the three rules of a family that do not function well: don't talk, don't trust and don't *feel*.

Acknowledging emotions does not mean you necessarily have to agree with them, but emotions can notify you of needs which God may expect you to address. For example, when Terry came home from work late one evening, he noticed his ten-year-old son was still up and was angry. His first inclination was to send the son to his bedroom until he could correct his bad attitude. But Terry had just finished a parenting refresher course at his church. Instead of the normal banishment routine he asked his son to sit down. Dad acknowledged his son's anger. He reassured him that while the emotion was all right, the important thing was what he did with it. Terry asked his son why he was angry. No answer. He tried again. Same response. His son was no dummy. Terry had gone off on him in the past, shamed him and overcorrected him.

It took a few more attempts before his son could trust his dad with his anger. "You promised me we would go shopping for my trail bike after dinner but now it's too late. You never keep your promises." Ouch! Yes, Terry did come home late. Yes, he did forget the promise to his son and yes, his son was hurt. Most immature parents would launch into a defense, minimize the child's feelings and then scold him for his bad attitude. Terry chose to do the right thing. He acknowledged his son's hurt feelings and thanked him for sharing them even though it was hard. A wise parent will admit his mistake and ask his child for forgiveness. You may be thinking that's not real life. You're right. To most people the *wrong* way feels right. God's way sounds strange. God tells us that His ways of dealing with life are not our ways. In fact, they are worlds apart (Isa. 55:8-9), but doing things His way brings His peace to your home.

Another source of anger is telling someone that he should *not* feel a certain way. It encourages him to lie about his true feelings. When feelings are stuffed down inside they can lead to depression or erupt in anger later.

Feelings respond to events. In his book, *The Other Side of Love*, Dr. Gary Chapman suggests that anger is always stimulated by an event in life (p. 18). Reflect on this statement, "The more I think about it (event), the angrier I get (emotions)." What comes first, thoughts or feelings? Rather than shaming, manipulating or chiding someone for his feelings, let his feelings act as a red light on his emotional dashboard, notifying you of a need. Terry did this with his son. He first acknowledged his son's feelings, then, explored the need behind them.

People are more likely to forgive and move on when there is an honest recognition of a wrong *and* a sincere effort to correct it. Your failure to acknowledge their hurt feelings only keeps them emotionally stuck at the point of the hurt. Shaming them for having those emotions deepens the heart-felt anger and ensures bitterness.

Telling family members how they should feel without addressing the issues behind the emotion is futile and leads to alienation. Why? The alienated one will conclude the other person does not care enough to discover what is behind these feelings or that he would not understand if an effort was made to explain them.

In allowing each family member to express normal emotions, we must distinguish between wrong attitudes and appropriate feelings.

Appropriate Feelings	Wrong Attitudes
Anger	Critical
Fear	Demeaning
Sadness	Sarcasm
Joy	Disrespect
Loneliness	Pouting
Dread	Bitterness

If Terry's son had said he was angry at his dad and then had called him a "*jerk*," the anger would have been appropriate but the name-calling would have been disrespectful. Terry was wise to separate the two issues. First he admitted his own failure to keep his promise and then he dealt appropriately with his son's negative emotions. If he had reversed this he would have lost big time. Jesus made it clear it was important to remove the beam (offense) that is in your own eye first. Then you will see clearly how to deal with the splinter in another's eye (Matt. 7:3-5).

REPLACE FEAR WITH TRUST

Over-protection and over-control reveals a lack of trust in someone outside of yourself, including God. One of the most frightening experiences I had as a parent occurred when Michelle was only three. Our family was frantically trying to finish some last-minute Christmas shopping in a packed mall. While walking through the crowd I inadvertently let go of her hand for what seemed a split second. I had been distracted and when I turned around to take her hand she was gone. To this very day I can still feel the terror that shot through my entire body. I glanced in every direction and could not see her. Which way did she go? I don't really remember the next few minutes. I only recall crying out to God - no, screaming out to God, "Which way should I go?"

After what seemed like an eternity I headed to the right and spotted a security guard about twenty feet away. Because of the crowd I could only see his head and shoulders as he began to walk toward me. Just as I was about to cry out for his help my eye dropped to his side. There, firmly clutching his hand, was Michelle. Relief and gratitude engulfed me.

As I praised God for Michelle's safe return He brought to mind the verse, "Unless the Lord guards the city the watchman keeps awake in vain" (Psalm 127:1). The light from the watchman's torch on the city wall only illuminates about fifty feet away from the wall. Beyond that is the blackness of night. An enemy could lurk in that darkness and launch an attack before the watchman could fully sound the alarm. God does not suggest the watchman cease his vigilance. It is his job to watch diligently. The protection of a city or a family comes not only from vigilance but ultimately trust in God because "He knows what is in the darkness" (Dan. 2:22).

Controlling spouses and parents factor God out and feel everything is totally up to them. This lack of trust in God produces fear that He may allow them to experience pain as Job did (Job 1:13-19). In their pursuit of a pain-free life they try to manage others out of fear.

Exasperating your children, spouse, friends or co-workers is never done out of faith, only fear. The resulting anger in either you or them is God's notifier that you may need to make a shift from fear and control to faith and freedom. How? Read Proverbs 3:5-6 slowly, "Trust in the Lord with all your heart and do not lean on your own understanding. In all your ways acknowledge Him and He will make your paths straight."

Fear is a faith substitute. It does not please God. "For without faith it is impossible to please God. For we must believe that He is (exists in our lives) and that He is a rewarder of those who diligently seek Him (factor Him into their daily lives)" (Heb. 11:5). Result? Faith moves God's peace first in your heart, then, in your relationships.

ANGER REDUCTION KEYS

1. Recognize that provoking a family member is sin and choose to stop it.
2. Change authoritative commands to respectful requests.
3. Eliminate perpetual fault-finding and excessive interference.
4. Identify and seek to heal damaged emotions.
5. Encourage age-appropriate choices.
6. Distinguish between moral issues, personal tastes and preferences.
7. Allow others to learn from their wrong choices.
8. Do not use shame to control or motivate.
9. Encourage the open expression of opinions.
10. Create a safe environment for expressing normal emotions.
11. Replace unhealthy fear with trust in God.

SMALL GROUP DISCUSSION QUESTIONS

1. Describe occasions when you were personally provoked or exasperated by an authority figure. How did you feel? How did it affect your behavior? How do you wish that person had handled it differently?

2. When someone orders you to do something instead of asking you, what does it convey? How does respect figure into this process?

3. When you were growing up did you live with criticism? What impact did it have on your life? How did it cause you to stumble in later years?

4. How do you feel when someone does not respect your boundaries or space?

5. If you lived in a controlling environment what kind of emotions did you struggle with? How did you deal with those emotions? How effective were your efforts?

6. When have you felt hopeless in situations beyond your control? How were you able to get through this effectively?

7. Describe times you were not permitted to make your own choices. How did it affect you?

8. What conflicts have you experienced with others between moral issues and personal taste? Where does a believer's freedom start and end?

9. What have you learned from mistakes in your life? How are you a better person today as a result of these mistakes?

10. How do you feel when you are around a highly opinionated person? What does that do to any relationship?

11. What emotions have you suppressed in your life? How did it happen? How were you able to regain the use of normal emotions?

12. Share your own personal journey of learning to replace fear with trust. How did you do it? What difference has it made in your life today?

SECTION III
SOURCES OF FRUSTRATION AND ANGER
IN THE FAMILY

CHAPTER 5

FAVORITISM, THE GRANDDADDY OF ANGER

FRED COULD SELL refrigerators to Eskimos. His charismatic, fun-loving personality made him the life of the party but this, of course, is not what brought Fred to my office for counseling. Parts of his life were not working. It did not take long for Fred to open up the dark inner room of his heart. He hated himself. He loathed everything about himself. His voice, height, weight, looks, hair; each feature screamed at him, *"Dumb, fat, and ugly."*

I featured Fred in our first book; *I Should Forgive, But. . .* Fred hated his alcoholic dad. He refused to forgive him until he understood that letting his dad off his hook put him on God's hook (Rom. 12:19). Fred realized it was not smart to keep his dad in the jail of his own heart so he delivered him over to the Lord to deal with him.

Right in the middle of Fred's painful monologue portraying his father's abuse, he glanced out my office window and in a hushed voice intoned, "I wish I was a girl." Jerking his head back toward me with a piercing stare he asserted, "Don't worry. I'm not weird."

Before I could respond to either statement he injected this bit of history. "My younger sister was the apple of my father's eye. She could do no wrong. I could do no right." Fred went on to paint a painful portrait of a father who delighted in his only daughter and viewed his only son as a competitor to defeat and control in every competition. This left Fred angry at his dad and himself.

Siblings secretly resent the favored one but desperately aspire to become the favorite to get their share of attention. They reach adulthood with a large chunk of hurt, resentment, shame and guilt that has accumulated over the years

ROOTS OF FAVORITISM

Favoritism, as played out by Fred's dad, would be easy to explain if the cutest, smartest, most athletic child was always singled out to be favored by the parent but this may not be the case. This should be a clue as to the real source of favoritism. But first let's clarify what we mean by favoritism. Favoritism means preferring one person *above* another at the *expense* of another. It tends to be expressed by isolating and concentrating special attention or delight on one or more persons to the exclusion of others.

Boys may be favored over girls or in Fred's case, just the opposite, so we know that gender differences alone are not the root of favoritism. Athletes may be preferred over musicians. We have seen the cute child favored over the plain child. Yet in some instances the pretty child is shunned for the more average one. Some parents prefer outgoing children; others like the quiet ones. One parent may prefer the dependent child while another parent is drawn to the more free-spirited child. A mother praises the compliant sibling and recoils at the strong-willed child. Yet in the same family the rebel could be the father's favorite. The slender child could be preferred over a chubby one. Add to this mix, "*his*" kids are favored over "*her*" kids in the blended family.

IT'S NOT ABOUT THE CHILD

By now we begin to see a pattern. Although more popular traits such as looks, personality and ability usually define the popular, likeable child, something else really becomes obvious: favoritism is not about the child. It is all about the parent.

The one key element in all expressions of favoritism is how a particular child makes the parent feel. It's a preference issue and how a particular child makes the adult feel. It is really about the parent, not the child, although the disfavored child may become very angry at a favored sibling because of it. Adults can use children to fill a void in their lives and kids will gladly cooperate in filling that void. Psychologist Dr. John Friel explains it this way, "Children are little air molecules who will swoop in and fill whatever vacuum they find. If your life is a vacuum, they'll automatically try to rush in and fill it up, no matter what you tell them to the contrary" (*The Seven Worst Things*, p. 95).

Favoritism is allowing one child to fill the parent's vacuum over another child. Adults may have a favorite because they may find it too difficult to develop adult relationships, especially with their spouse. Since kids are dependent they return love and are less likely to leave us if we hurt them. It is all about how a particular child makes the parent *feel*, not what the child *needs*. God documented this sad reality with a patriarchal father's dying wish.

THE FOOD OF FAVORITISM

Life was drawing to a close for the Old Testament patriarch, Isaac. He felt the chilling north wind of death approaching. He desired one last pleasure and only his favorite son, Esau, could provide it. Esau had a twin brother, Jacob. Favoritism between the twins was the occasion that split the marriage emotionally between their parents, Isaac and Rebekah. Dad loved Esau. Mom loved Jacob (Gen. 25:28). Look closely at the selfish reason Isaac favored Esau, "Now Isaac loved Esau because he had a taste for game..." Esau was a wild game hunter.

There is nothing wrong in and of itself with enjoying the taste of wild game as many seasoned hunters can attest. That is not the issue. It is when Isaac placed more value on Esau than his brother Jacob, based solely on Esau's ability to provide his dad his favorite wild game dishes rather than viewing each person as God does without partiality (Acts 10:34).

It was not Esau's fault that his dad favored him, nor was it Jacob's fault that his mom loved him more than his brother. God had revealed to Rebekah before their births the roles the twins were to live out. It was a sovereign choice of a holy God. Isaac knew the oracle clearly declared by God to his wife that "the older (Esau) shall serve the younger" (Jacob) (Gen. 25:23). But in sheer disregard of God while pandering to his own palate, Isaac wanted one more personal pleasure before death came knocking - a wild game stew. That was not wrong in itself. However, Isaac was going to give the family blessing to Esau because he brought his father pleasure while ignoring the command of God. Personal appetite was about to defy God's sovereign choice.

The unfolding of Jacob's deception of his father and "stealing" the family blessing ultimately devastated the family. When Esau learned that there was no blessing for him, he "lifted up his voice and wept" (Gen. 27:38). It got worse. Esau bore a bitter grudge against Jacob and consoled himself by reasoning, "The days of mourning for my father are near; then I will kill my brother Jacob" (Gen. 27:41).

Rebekah alerted her favorite son Jacob of the murderous plot and manipulated her husband into sending Jacob to her brother Laban to find a wife. The family rift was so severe that Jacob never saw his mother again. The son of her love was never to grace and delight her presence again.

This parental favoritism ultimately tore the family completely apart. Again, favoritism is never shown for the benefit of the child. It is always based on the selfish pleasure of the parent. Bitterness is the adult that favoritism raised.

EVERY CHILD, A UNIQUE DESIGN

In our travels I have spent more than my fair share of time waiting in airports. I enjoy watching people. One thing is obvious, no two people are alike. Everyone is different, uniquely designed by creator God. King David gave us a glimpse into God's workshop, "For Thou didst form my inward part; Thou didst weave me in my mother's womb. I will give thanks to Thee for I am fearfully and wonderfully made; wonderful are Thy works, and my soul knows it very well. My frame was not hidden from Thee, when I was made in secret, and skillfully wrought in the depths of the earth. Thine eyes have seen my unformed substance; and in Thy book they were all written, the days that were ordained for me, when as yet there was not one of them" (Ps. 139:13-16). Everyone is different. Although there are many similar characteristics, each person is a one-of-a-kind design.

The word "Thou," referring to God, is very emphatic in the Hebrew language. Favoritism factors God out of the relational process. Most of us will give a mental ascent to the popular motto, "God does not make any junk," but favoritism ignores the worth God places on each person. Favoritism is essentially a slap in the face of God for it devalues God's workmanship (Eph. 2:10). The selfish practice of favoritism virtually dismisses from the mind the sovereignty of God in creating a life through the natural processes of procreation.

It may be easy with just an elementary understanding of the facts of life to dismiss any of God's responsibility in creating a child, especially in the tragic cases of rape or incest. Each child, however conceived, is uniquely designed by God and deserves protection. The fact that each person is an exhibition of God's creative workmanship should prompt praise back to God the Father (Ps. 139: 14), not pander to selfish pleasure of favorites and thus physically or emotionally destroy the life God is creating.

King David reflecting on the rich tapestries adorning his palace walls, made an incredible comparison. He declared that each child is woven together (literally "embroidered" together) like a finely made tapestry. I had the opportunity to examine both sides of an ornately woven tapestry while in Egypt. The underside is definitely less attractive while the right side is a thing of beauty. As we look at the tapestry of our lives we may see only the tangled underside of losses, hurts and pain. God sees how these are adding to the beauty of the topside. Favoritism assesses a person's value from below, not from above.

Honestly I *have* to trust that God really is at work in some people's lives. With my finite perspective I choose to trust God that each one is highly valued and masterfully woven. I must resist my internal urge to measure a person's value by how he makes me *feel*. Instead, you and I both must ask how this creation of God makes Him *feel*. Seeing each person from God's perspective greatly reduces the possibility of anger and increases the potential for family peace. Failure to do so will only inflame anger in the family.

Finally King David relates that "in Your book they were all written the days that were ordained for me when as yet there was not one of them" (Ps. 139:16). This could either refer to the length of his life or to the day-by-day plan for his life. Either way they are parts of a whole. Duration and destiny are inseparable.

Each member of your family was uniquely designed for a specific plan by a sovereign God. He grieves when you devalue or despise any one of them. Favoritism virtually dismisses God's plan for each child while selfishly obsessing on how a particular child makes you feel. No wonder favoritism breaks the heart of God and enrages the family member that is devalued. Rejection spawned by favoritism is excruciatingly painful. Murder in homes, schools and churches is its heritage.

A DIFFERENT CHILD, A DIFFERENT FAMILY

On October 17, 1968, a beautiful daughter was born to Linda and me. It was an incredible experience. I was in the delivery room when she was born. A few years later we wanted a baby brother or sister. Two, three, then four years passed with many disappointments.

By the time DeeDee was thirteen we moved from the Chicago area to Kansas City. I had hardly begun a college teaching and administrative career when Linda announced she was pregnant. Surprise! God gave us another beautiful daughter.

The family dynamics drastically changed. Our second child was born into a different family than our first. Although children may have the same parents, no two children are born into the same family. DeeDee was born into a family of two. Later, Michelle was born into a family of three.

Family dynamics change as each new child arrives. This change has the potential for favoritism. The first child gets the total attention of the new, excited parents. Each developmental stage is eagerly anticipated such as first steps and first words. The second child may receive a little less attention. When the third child arrives the now seasoned parents may give little thought to each of the child's developmental stages. It takes a special effort to remember that each child is unique and is born into a different family while possessing the same biological parents.

Parents also mellow with age. Linda and I changed from rigid parents to more relaxed parents over time. Things that were absolutely essential years before became less crucial as we aged. We got upset over fewer things. We were different. We had grown up too. That wasn't the problem. Anger enters the picture when each child sees our different parenting style, skills and responses over time and concludes there is favoritism in the family.

Blended families can face a slightly different challenge than traditional families. The children of the step father may feel their step mother treats her kids differently than them. A little honesty could help tremendously here. The reality is that the mom will always love and feel a deeper attachment to the children she birthed than the ones that joined the family by marriage. The same is true for the dad.

The key is that each child should get equal honor and respect by both parents although the parents' emotional attachment will vary. I personally feel it is unreasonable for a step parent to expect his new spouse to love his kids as deeply as he does. If it happens, fine. Nevertheless, it *is* reasonable to expect the same honor and respect to be exhibited to each member in the home.

It is absolutely crucial that when any child brings their perception differences to our attention that we do not defend ourselves. Listen to their feelings and acknowledge the reality of those feelings and ask, "What do you need now?" Do not defend, lecture, belittle or chide them for their jealousy and immaturity. Please do not tell them they should not feel that way. Their emotions are the signs of the needs. Listening, understanding and making honest adjustments will go a long way toward reducing the anger that comes from what they perceive as partiality and favoritism. Failure to do this can sow many seeds of anger that will produce a crop of bitterness in the children for years to come.

DIFFERENT CHILD, DIFFERENT INCLINATION

In my earlier years I had the privilege of being a youth pastor in West Covina, California. That ministry experience is one of the highlights of my life. Twenty-six years later at a youth group reunion over 160 of the "*kids*" showed up with their families and pictures of their children and grandchildren.

I recall something I heard years ago from a few of their parents that gave me some insight into their parenting style. They would say, "I treat all my children just the same." That was usually shared with a tinge of pride. But I noticed that youth from families with that philosophy were usually unhappy campers. When their individual interests, abilities and needs were ignored anger took root. Each child must be reared according to his or her own uniquely designed bent. Each child must also be taught to respect each other's uniqueness but the instruction from you must be preceded by your modeling of that respect.

God created us with different inclinations psychologically, emotionally, physically and vocationally. Solomon reflected this reality, "Train up a child in the way he should go, even when he is old he will not depart from it" (Proverbs 22:6). Scholars are divided on whether this refers to vocational, moral or personality bents. A strong case could be made for any or all of the three. I personally believe there are strands of truth in each.

A great deal of anger is injected into a son who is gifted in mechanics but is shamed because he has no interest in college or books. He's a "*hands on*"kid. If his siblings go to college and he does not, guess who is highly favored and who is discounted in value?

During my time as a college instructor I saw many students who would have been better off in a technical institute or vocational training school instead of a Christian college. I watched young men who were "preordained" by their parents to be pastors or missionaries but who did not have the slightest calling. To the few students who were open, I suggested that they follow their interests or desires that God put in their hearts. Today one of my former students is a very successful tool salesman. He developed his own company and is a dynamic leader in his local church. He is the first to admit he would have made a poor pastor.

Chip came to me totally bewildered as to what he should do with his life. He started college as an electrical engineer and hated it. But he had to do it; his dad made it clear that was the only way to be financially secure in the future. The classes became progressively more difficult. Fear gripped his heart. Failure in engineering meant rejection and disappointment at home. The inevitable happened. He flunked three courses. It was then that he changed his major to journalism and did quite well. There was one small problem. In his father's eyes he was a failure. Chip wrestled with rejection and, quite honestly, anger. Chip's vocational interest and his parents' approval collided. Even now as he finishes an additional degree in theology and desires to be a self-supporting missionary, he still struggles emotionally feeling his dad's disappointment. Chip had to honestly face the reality that the father's disappointment was his father's issue; not his. His dad could only feel good about himself if Chip was an electrical engineer.

Months later I met his aging father. He had mellowed. He had learned to want Chip's happiness whatever his calling. I thought of all the pain and resulting anger that could have been avoided if that perspective was in play years earlier.

I have known medical doctors who hated medicine but the family expected them to be doctors. I have seen the same with lawyers, farmers and owners of family-run businesses. Low-grade anger continues and simmers because the parent or family "needed" their son or daughter to be something they were never designed by God to be. Remember, favoritism never happens for the benefit of the child. It happens for the pleasure or need of the parent or family. Forcing a child into an area that God did not design him for is not for the benefit of the child. A child not reared according to his God-designed bent will in later years break. Anger and bitterness will be seen in the smoldering ruins of his life. There will be little peace in that house.

Every son or daughter is different and must be treated accordingly but always from mature and impartial love. God deals differently with the ungodly and godly. The ungodly He desires to lead to salvation and the godly to growth in holiness. Two different divine strategies acknowledge these differences. However, both issue forth from His incredible love and impartiality (John 3:16).

WHY IS GOD IMPARTIAL?

There are at least five reasons God does not show partiality. These are the very same reasons you should not show partiality through favoritism.

IMAGE BEARERS

First, each person was created in the image of God (Gen. 1:27). Although "image" is used figuratively, because God is a Spirit, we do share in His likeness in many ways. We have communicable attributes: love, wisdom, reason, truth, holiness, justice and the capacity for fellowship with God. These set us totally apart from the rest of creation. True, the image is now distorted through sin but it is not erased. Favoritism fails to honor the unique image-bearing reality in each person and incites anger in the family.

DIVINE PURPOSE

Second, each person, whether righteous or unrighteous, was created for a specific purpose. "All things have been created *by* Him and *for* Him… and in Him all things hold together" (Col.1:16). Our Lord Jesus Christ created everything. He holds it all together today as always. It was created and is being held together for Him and His purposes.

A son or daughter may appear to us to be just drifting without any purpose, especially when they "veg out" for hours mindlessly in front of the TV or only seem to be preoccupied with their music. But a holy God still loves them and chooses to show no partiality. He longs to fill their life with meaning and purpose.

God even uses the wicked to accomplish His purposes. When Israel rebelled God said he would *whistle* for the pagan nations of the world (Egypt, Assyria, and later Babylon) to come and destroy Judah because of her great sin (Isa. 5:26). God even calls the wicked Babylonian king, Nebuchadnezzar, "My servant" (Jer. 43:10). God has a purpose for all. To show favoritism is to ignore God's sovereign purpose for even the most insignificant person. Favoritism factors God out of our perspective, devalues another person, sows the seeds of anger and drains God's peace from our homes. There is no genuine peace apart from the character of God reflected by those in our home.

PART OF A WHOLE

Third, God is impartial because He knows each person is an important part of a whole. He confronted the church in Corinth for showing favoritism to people who possessed certain gifts of the Spirit. Paul uses a word picture of the human body to describe the structure of the church. As the human body is a unit, so is the body of Christ. Just as the body has many parts, so there is diversity in the church. As the different parts of the human body function as one, so should believers in the body of Christ (I Cor.12:12).

The birth family is to be the first expression of this word picture of the body of Christ. There is to be diversity in the family yet it is to function as a unit. Paul then addresses two ingredients that destroy that unity. The first is inferiority. "If the foot says, 'Because I am not a hand, I am not part of the body,' it is not for this reason any less a part of the body" (I Cor. 12:15). The issue here is that a person feels disconnected and less valued than another part of the church body. This may have been the result of people minimizing or ignoring their importance to the whole body.

Then Paul addresses the second ingredient that destroys unity: superiority. "And the eye cannot say to the hand, 'I have no need of you,' or again the head to the feet, 'I have no need of you'" (I Cor. 12:21). Favoritism that excludes anyone from the family leads to self-deception and the lie that one is better off without that person. Such an attitude blatantly ignores two realities. First, God is the one who sovereignly placed them there (I Cor. 12:18). Secondly, if the truth were known, the members of the body (family) which seem to be weaker or inferior are more necessary.

I have witnessed those who chose to honor a severely handicapped sibling become healthy adults with compassion and character, appreciating the uniqueness of each life. But I have also witnessed others who devalued or dishonored a family member and fought shame and guilt the rest of their lives.

The bottom line is, "Those members of the body which we deem (think) less honorable, on these we bestow more abundant honor" (I Cor. 12:23). The emotionally and spiritually mature parent who senses a family member struggling with inferiority will show them more honor and respect. This conveys God's value to them as a vital part of the family. Peace will replace anger.

HIS INCREDIBLE LOVE

The fourth reason God does not show partiality is simply because He loves everyone. The most quoted verse in the Bible makes that reality clear, "For God so loved the world, (no exceptions) that He gave His only begotten Son, that whoever believes in Him should not perish but have eternal life" (John 3:16). Every child is different and has to be treated differently. That treatment must come from impartial love.

One of the most damaging lies imaginable produces an emotion which says, "I feel unloved because I think I am unlovable." This is a lie from the pit of hell that becomes firmly rooted early in life. I know. I've experienced it.

I was raised in my earlier years in an alcoholic home. My father was never physically or verbally abusive to me or my two brothers. He did something more damaging. When I was in my early teens my dad completely abandoned the family. He disappeared. He sent no money home for our maintenance. He left the entire burden on my mother to financially support the family. That was one thing. But something deeper happened. The meaning I attached to my father's abandonment was, "He does not love me." I then wrongly concluded I must not be lovable. For years I lived with the lie that I was unlovable. My father's abandonment inflicted incredible emotional damage on me that made me feel unlovable.

If the oceans of the world could not contain enough ink to tell of the love of God, then all the lakes of the world could not contain enough ink to tell of the anger and emotional damage the lies favoritism can cause.

HE JUDGES RIGHTEOUSLY

Finally, God does not show partiality in how He judges. Isaiah describes the coming Messiah, "He will not judge by what His eyes see, nor make a decision by what His ears hear" (Isa. 11:3). He will judge on the basis of what is right. If the King of kings dealt with me according to what He sees me doing or hears me saying from time to time, I would be dog meat. Why does He show us more mercy than we deserve? In part it is because we are His image bearers. He has a specific purpose for each of our lives. We are a valuable part of a bigger picture. We are incredibly loved. He does not show favoritism by what He sees in us and hears from us but chooses rather to grant us mercy out of His unfathomable grace.

COMPARISON, THE CULPRIT

"Chip!" His name rang out in disgust, "Why can't you just be like your brother? What's wrong with you anyway?" His dad let out a perturbed sigh, then stomped out of the room slamming the door behind him. Another son damaged. Another father lacking understanding. There is a simple answer to his father's question. Chip cannot be just like his brother because Chip is *not* his brother. He has different interests, abilities and personality but he just does not fit Dad's predetermined game plan for his life. The sad part is that his dad does not realize that it has nothing to do with Chip. It has everything to do with him. The Apostle Paul confronted this very issue with the Corinthian believers.

THE WISE BECAME FOOLS

Paul faced pointed opposition to his ministry in Corinth. These Jewish Christians believed that they were themselves the apostles of Christ (2 Cor.10:7). They brought letters from others with glowing recommendations (2 Cor. 3:1) and indulged in prideful self-aggrandizement (2 Cor. 10:18). They drew their prominence from identifying themselves with the so-called "super apostles." How did Paul deal with this arrogant elitism?

First, he attacked their human value system of comparing themselves with each other. Their selective amnesia ignored God's holy standard role-modeled by Christ. They adopted human standards to convey godly values.

Second, Paul hits the fact head on that human standards of comparison and value do not reflect divine wisdom but rather human foolishness. The so-called "wisdom of the world" is marked by jealousy, selfish ambition, pride and deceit. It is secular, unspiritual and yes, demonic (James 3:14,15). The fruit of this Satan inspired "wisdom" is all kinds of disorder and evil practices. One of these is favoritism. When *parents* place a higher value on one child than another they are not reflecting God's perspective but an earthly one controlled by the prince of the power of the air, Satan.

Most of us want a better quality of life and spiritual maturity in our lives than we may have experienced in our birth families.

If the disorder, confusion and ungodly practices within our homes were known publicly, it would devastate us with shame.

Favoritism and ungodly comparisons are evil practices, commonplace in the Christian home that rob us of the peace we greatly desire. By adopting the following keys to reducing anger you will indeed experience God's peace in your home.

ANGER REDUCTION KEYS

1. Honestly admit the ways you have demonstrated favoritism in the family.
2. Confess to those to whom you have hurt that your demonstration of favoritism had nothing to do with them. It was a selfish perspective on your part. Ask for forgiveness.
3. Accept as your core belief that every member of your family is a God-designed person with weaknesses and strengths.
4. Determine to appreciate all the beautiful God-designed persons in your family from His perspective.
5. Trust God to use each family member with the "bent" He created them to have.
6. Grant to each member of the family the gift of grace (favor) just as God did to you.
7. Admit to yourself that you and your children have changed through the years and make allowances for that change.
8. Refuse to use any member of your family to increase your place of prominence in the home, church or community.
9. Demonstrate a mature love to each member of your family.
10. Help each family member to fit into the whole program God has for the family and the church and the world.
11. Stop comparing and start commending the uniqueness you see in each other.

SMALL GROUP DISCUSSION QUESTIONS

1. Describe what you experienced when favoritism was shown to others.
2. What possible pleasure did the one demonstrating favoritism receive? How appropriate do you feel it was?
3. How has God enabled you to love and accept someone that others have devalued?
4. How did the dynamics of your home change with the addition of each new sibling, including adoption and remarriage?
5. What pressures were applied by parents or others for you to do or become something different than what you wanted? How did you deal with this in later life? How do you wish it had been handled differently?
6. What pain have you experienced or witnessed from unfavorable comparison? What do you feel was the purpose of that unfavorable comparison? Did it accomplish its goal? What lasting effect did it have?
7. Have you come to accept God's design for your life in all areas? What events, persons and scripture helped you to accomplish this?

CHAPTER 6

REJECTION, DEVALUED IN ANGER

THE HOT AFTERNOON sun radiated off the asphalt basketball court at my junior high school. The blistering southern California heat was bad but I would soon experience something worse. It was time to choose sides for intramural basketball in our gym class. Coach Woodburn selected two guys to act as captains. Each one took turns picking the best players to form two squads. I hated it!

In junior high I had developed a thyroid problem that resulted in obesity. I felt I was as wide as I was tall. My theme song was, "Roly Poly, Daddy's Little Fatty, He is Going to be a Man Someday." Being fat was not the worst part. As the captains took turns choosing sides, the player pool shrunk until I was the only one left.

I would hide in the back of the class pretending I wasn't chosen because they just didn't see me. Yes, I was in denial but I always knew I would be last. Finally, the whole experience took its toll.

One afternoon I ran into my bedroom and sprawled across my bed, sobbing. Mom followed me into my room. She saw something was wrong.

Mom took me to the Gallatin Medical Clinic where I was given thyroid medicine and put on a medically supervised diet. I lost 50 pounds and I grew almost a foot in one year. Although I balanced out physically early in high school and even played a little football, I carried a deep emotional scar. Its effects are with me to this day, the dreaded fear of re-feeling the pain of that rejection.

The pain from rejection is expressed in horrific ways in society. Almost all the ex-husbands and ex-boyfriends who have killed their former spouses or lovers were angry over being rejected. The public school massacres of scores of innocent students are partially fueled by peer rejection, not the failure of gun control laws.

Ahithophel, one of the seven suicides recorded in scripture, killed himself in response to rejection (2 Sam. 17:23). The first murder in history was rooted in Cain's anger over God's rejection of him for failing to offer the appropriate sacrifice (Gen. 4:5). The Jewish feast of Purim was occasioned by Queen Esther's intervention of Haman's evil plot to kill all the Jewish people. He hated Mordecai, the Jew, because he refused to bow down to him. That one rejection led to a series of events that destroyed Haman and his entire family (Esther 3:2b).

One of the most dangerous forms of anger in the family comes from the feeling of rejection. The fear of rejection is perhaps the most dreaded emotion known to mankind.

WHAT IS REJECTION?

I was asked to speak at a church in central Pennsylvania, rich in Colonial history. In preparing the message I found myself stretching to come up with a visual illustration of rejection. Halfway through the message that Sunday morning my eyes glanced at a copy of the church bulletin on the pulpit. Someone spent a lot of time collecting the information and designing an attractive layout. It was a valuable communications tool in the church.

"That's it," I thought. When I got to the part in my message where Jesus experienced rejection by His own people (John 1:12), I picked up the quality designed church bulletin. As I held it up I affirmed that it was a valuable piece of material. I recalled from my own pastoral experience what it took to put one together and print it. It helped us stay on track for the morning service. Then I abruptly took the lovely bulletin, crumpled it into a ball and threw it into the audience.

Eyes widened in shock. I went on to explain to the congregation that our English word, "rejection," means "to throw back." It implies that someone has picked up something, regarded it as worthless and in disdain threw it back to the one who offered it for approval. God used the same word picture to describe Jeroboam's rejection of Himself, " . . . you have gone and made for yourself other gods and molten images to provoke Me to anger and have *cast Me behind your back*" (I Kings 14:9).

The Greek word for rejection, *apodokimzo,* in essence means to reject after examination and disapproval. Our Lord and Savior, Jesus Christ, was likewise examined, disapproved of and rejected by the chief priests, scribes and elders of Israel. He was then tried and declared innocent seven times, then killed by the political Roman establishment (Mark 8:31).

Rejection has at least *three* aspects. First, you make something that is of worth and value to you. Second, someone picks it up, evaluates it and concludes it is worthless. Third, it is thrown back to you in disdain. This is rejection.

How painful it is when someone rejects what we have poured our time and energy into creating. I have had my share of publishers' rejection letters. Best-selling author, Max Lucado, told me he was rejected fifteen times before his first book was accepted for publication. Frank Peretti experienced over twenty-five rejections before his first book was published. Rejection of your created object is one thing. That's painful. But it does not hold a candle to the gut-wrenching pain of being the object of rejection, thrown back in disdain. Anger from this form of rejection is the most devastating and dangerous anger in the family and society.

FAILED SAFE HAVENS

I believe God designed two safe havens in life - the home and the church. It is not within the scope of this book to address the acceptance/rejection patterns played out in church politics. After fifty years of ministry I have seen more than my fair share of this. My focus is the believer's home. How can we reduce anger rooted in rejection in the Christian home?

A young person stood in the lobby of our ministry office perusing the bookshelf. Her eyes fell on Dr. Margaret Rinck's book, *Christian Men Who Hate Women*. She asked me a very pointed question as she walked to the door, "How can a man be a Christian and hate women?" It is the same question I ask regarding rejection in the believer's home, "How can you reject your wife, husband, son or daughter and have any trace of God's Spirit in you?" The sad reality is that it does exist. If anger reveals rejecting patterns in your home, how can they be corrected? Let's start with what we mean by acceptance.

FOUNDATION FOR ACCEPTANCE

It has been a number of years since I sat in my homiletics class under Dr. Glen O'Neal. In this sermon preparation class Dr. O'Neal explained to us young preachers where to go for resources in scripture for special occasions such as Father's Day. I will never forget his apologetic demeanor as he shared that there are very few examples in scripture of fathers acting in a godly way toward their children.

"Dr. O'Neal must be wrong," I thought. The Bible had to be filled with illustrations of fathers who were godly examples to their children. So I began my personal pilgrimage from Genesis to Revelation. To my dismay my research confirmed what my esteemed professor stated. There are scarcely any examples in scripture of godly home environments. True, there are many godly men and women in the Bible. The writer of Hebrews delineates many of them in Hebrews 11 in God's faith hall of fame

My research led me through the systematic theology in the book of Romans. There I saw God's standard for how we are to accept others. It was not exactly what I expected. God does not command us to accept one another just like Abraham accepted Isaac or David accepted Solomon. God simply says, "...accept one another *just as Christ* also accepted us to the glory of God" (Romans 15:7). The verb "*to accept*" can be translated "*keep on accepting*." This is a command, not advice.

To reject someone through your words, behavior or attitude directly violates God's expressed will. If you have stopped accepting your spouse or your children you are violating this command. The words, "*one another,*" leave no room for an exception. Jesus received those who were "p*owerless*" (Rom. 5:8), who were weak and even out of control. He welcomed the "*ungodly*" (Rom. 5:6) who were totally void of any godly character. Our Lord took a lot of heat for receiving "sinners" (Rom. 5:8) who did not measure up or were totally missing the character target established by a holy God. If that were not enough Jesus even received His "enemies" (Rom. 5:10) who were bent on His destruction and failure. Our Lord's love was put on public display for us on the cross before we made one behavioral change (Rom. 5:8).

With Christ as the role model for acceptance of others, let's discuss practical ways to reduce anger caused by rejection and increase God's peace in your home.

PURPOSE TO ACCEPT LIKE CHRIST

Determine now before going any further that you are going to make one of the biggest paradigm shifts of your life. In the past your spouse or child may have been warmly accepted by you based on their favorable performance. Though that feels right, there is one small problem, it is *dead wrong*. To give acceptance based on a person's performance must stop today. Failure to make this heart change is an almost guaranteed set up for divorce or rebellion. Why? Rejection means you have determined the other person is of little or no value and you are throwing them back with disgust and disdain. No spouse or child can thrive with this attitude even in a so-called Christian home. Rejection is not Christian!

Each family member is to receive the same acceptance you received in God's family. Failure to do so sets them up to believe the lie that acceptance is only based on performance. It results in a deep anger toward the conditional parent which then gets transferred to God. The child or mate feels God is rejecting them also. I have seen countless adults who view God as mean, frowning on them and just waiting to clobber them at the slightest indiscretion or misstep.

If parents continue to demonstrate conditional love and performance-based acceptance, the kids will learn this pattern and reproduce it in their own "Christian" homes. The rejected child will often marry a person who rejects them, whose love is based on performance. You have not seen pain until you see your patterns reproduced in your children and acted out on your grandchildren. This is serious because performance-based approval is totally against the character of God while it fits nicely with Satan's strategy to further destroy the work of God in our lives.

Performance-based approval is so contrary to the character and plan of God that He dedicated the whole book of Galatians in the New Testament to address performance-based acceptance. Listen to how the Apostle Paul described it: "You foolish Galatians, who has bewitched you, before whose eyes Jesus Christ was publicly portrayed as crucified? This is the only thing I want to find out from you, did you receive the Spirit by the works (performance) of the Law or by hearing with faith (grace)? Are you so foolish? Having begun by the Spirit, are you now being perfected by the flesh (performance)?" (Gal. 3:1-3). Our Lord's acceptance of us was totally based on grace (Eph. 2: 8-9).

God encourages us to obey Him out of appreciation for our total acceptance through His unfathomable love and sacrifice (Rom. 12:1). Strive to accept and value every family member just as God receives you into His family. Avoid at all cost pushing your child or mate to perform for the sole purpose of gaining your approval. That pressure to perform will invariably result in anger. Decide in your heart to accept each member of your family just as Christ accepts them.

PRACTICE THE STOP – START PRINCIPLE

In counseling it is one thing to coach a counselee to stop a particular destructive pattern of life. It is quite another to replace it with a healthy attitude and behavioral pattern.

I can tell a husband to stop devastating his wife through criticism. When he does so she is relieved but that is not all she wanted. She wanted him to start encouraging her with appropriate praise. If you stop a negative pattern but fail to replace it with a positive one, it is only a matter of time before you will default back to the negative pattern.

Scripture describes the stop-start pattern this way, "In reference of your former manner (habits) of life, you lay aside the old self (stop) … and put on the new self (start), which in the likeness of God has been created in righteousness and holiness of the truth" (Eph. 4:22-24). The biblical pattern of correction is to stop doing something and replace it by doing something beneficial in its place.

This is how God corrects unloving behavior in His own family. Correction involves three simple steps: First, remember the many acts of love you used to do. Next, repent or stop practicing the unloving actions you have been doing. Finally, return to the daily habit of expressing Christ-like love to each other (Rev. 2:5). Since nature abhors a vacuum, starting new patterns is as important as stopping old ones.

GRANT ACCEPTANCE AS A GIFT

How do you relieve the pressure to perform for acceptance in the family? Shift the core belief of your heart from "*earn*" to "*give*."

Our daughter, Michelle, graduated from high school in the top 5% of her class. She never received a semester grade of a "B" in all of her years of schooling and even took a couple college credit classes in high school. Michelle was praised for all of her achievements in school, in church, in ministry, in missions and community service. As her parents we made sure one thing stayed consistent. She is loved and accepted for who she *is*, not what she *does*. Our acceptance of her is our gift to her.

In her day-to-day world she experienced more than her share of rejection by peers. We cried and prayed with her when friends shifted loyalties and would not invite her to "their" functions. We watched two of her closest friends abruptly turn on her during her junior year of high school. At the same time her first boyfriend stopped seeing her and talked negatively about her to their mutual friends. She was hurt but she had a core belief that kept her going. She always knew she was accepted for who she was (our daughter) not for what she did (her achievement).

Yes, we let her make mistakes and learn from them. She did not always use "our mature" judgment as an adolescent but through it all she has matured into a confident young woman - not because she always performed well but because she was secure in our acceptance.

You may rightly wonder that if she had gotten into drugs, immorality or rebellion, would we have been as accepting? Honestly, we never experienced this with either of our two daughters. I can tell you both her mother and I read and reread the parable of the prodigal son as our girls grew up. We both determined if they fell into that pattern they would face two deeply grieved parents whose love would not end. But we would also allow them to face the consequences of their behavior on the other hand. Both of the girls knew that if they honored the Lord, their parents and themselves, we would go to no end to make our family resources available to them for college, weddings and beyond. That is the reward for faithfulness. But even if they chose a sinful path, nothing they could do could change or alter in any way our love for them.

REWARD GOOD BEHAVIOR

Throughout the years Michelle demonstrated she could be trusted. She earned it. In contrast, favor and value are gifts to be granted as God grants them, not to be earned. However, trust is earned, not demanded. Trust-building behavior should be rewarded.

It was our joy to grant Michelle's heart's desire to visit her lifelong friend, Kristin, in Brazil, where her family were missionaries. Michelle has been very open to serving the Lord cross-culturally in a foreign environment. Her track record of responsibility was good. She earned trust that motivated us to reward her more than we would have normally done financially.

You may have a son or daughter who has repeatedly made bad choices. Out of his past track record of poor choices you may not be able to trust him. He may even attempt to manipulate you with the challenge, "You don't trust me!" How should you respond? Try saying, "Yes, you're right. We don't trust you. You have betrayed our trust with unwise decisions. We love you and deeply care for you. You are valued in our eyes because you are our son - a gift from God. I really look forward to working out a plan with you that will work for both of us to restore that trust."

You may be thinking, "Right! That will never work." But may I ask you a question? Has your yelling, screaming, name calling or shaming been effective for you? It is my personal opinion that God's way of granting the gift of honor to a difficult teenager is light years ahead of the shaming and demeaning by an angry parent. Grant honor as a gift. But reward good behavior just as God does to us as His children (Matt. 5:11-12).

ACCEPT IN FAILURE

Accept your spouse or child in love at their every point of failure. The popular story of the father of the prodigal son illustrates this in Luke 15:17-20. The younger of two sons requested of his father his half of the inheritance. He left home for a far country where he squandered it all. Destitute and broken, he humbly returned home. Humiliated by failure, he believed his worth was in his performance. He told his father, "I am no longer worthy to be called your son." Little did he know his father's heart. To his father, worth came with son-ship, not performance. Dad welcomed the repentant son home. Yes, there were consequences and losses because of the son's poor choices. However, just as Romans 15:7 clearly states, "Keep on receiving to yourself" (i.e. accepting) even those who have failed, sinned miserably or may have hurt you deeply. Your openness to accept the person back may be the fertile soil needed for the seeds of healing.

Acceptance does not mean automatic trust. Acceptance is recognition of a person's God-given intrinsic value. It also implies your willingness to go through the difficult experience of allowing him to rebuild the trust. You are now learning to trust all over again. It is tough, but it is worth it.

DISTINGUISH BETWEEN ACCEPTANCE AND APPROVAL

Anita was crushed to learn her only son was a homosexual. Words fail to describe the excruciating pain she endured while working through this crisis. Years later she was able to join forces with Bob Davies, the executive director of Exodus International, an agency to help men and women seek freedom from homosexuality, and to write the book, *Someone I Love is Gay.*

Both Bob and Anita go to the heart of a very difficult situation. Their answer addresses the hard question, "What do I do when someone I love is making wrong choices? If I accept him does it convey that I approve of his behavior?"

Bob and Anita's answer is simple but profound. Distinguish between acceptance and approval. These two words mean different things. *Acceptance* means "acknowledging what is true." It honestly recognizes the reality of a person's choice and behavior. Denial is not accepting reality. *Approval,* on the other hand, means "affirming something as good or right." It confirms a person's choices and behaviors are right.

It is very appropriate to tell someone that you accept or acknowledge the reality of what he is doing. Then to affirm your continued love for him, tell him you are hurt by his choices and you believe his choices are wrong. That's not the hard part. The next step is much harder.

Bob and Anita express it this way, "After clearly stating your position it's time to back off and simply love him. From then on he will know your stand on his actions" (p. 115). He may react to you and assert that if you reject his choices, you are rejecting him. That is his problem. He has failed to distinguish *who* he is from *what* he does.

The father of the prodigal son never approved of his son's behavior. He accepted the reality of the son's poor choices but never denied that he was still his son.

The Apostle Paul accepted the fact that the Corinthians were saints (1 Cor. 1:2) but he totally disapproved of their sectarianism (3:1-3), immorality (5:1-7), law suits between believers (6:1-8) and inappropriate conduct at the Lord's supper (11:17-22). You are not responsible for another person's choices, only for your attitude toward them. Distinguish between acceptance and approval.

VISUALIZE CORRECTED FAILURE

The only thing worse than a mistake is an uncorrected mistake. Your devaluing attitude of your spouse or child automatically disqualifies you from being part of the healing or correction.

Rejection means you have devalued someone or something and thrown it back in disgust. It's hard to hug a family member you just straight-armed. However, when you take on the attitude of the Lord Jesus (Rom. 13:14), and communicate your love, care and Christ's value of them, people are more apt to be open for you to be a part of their restoration.

With a Christ-like perspective you are now in a much better position to help visualize the correction of failure and its benefit for each child or mate. Jesus did this for the colossal failure, Peter. Jesus said to Peter, "Simon, Simon, behold, Satan has demanded permission to sift you like wheat" (Luke 22:31). Satan's goal was to get Peter to fail so badly that he would separate Peter from his faith and make him feel that God would never accept him back.

Jesus role modeled a response that must be applied in every family. He said, "But I have prayed for you that your faith may not fail, and you, when once you have turned again, strengthen your brothers" (Luke 22:32). I find this to be incredible! I can hear Jesus saying, "Peter, you are going to mess up big time. I know it. You are going to reject Me and how am I going to respond? I am drawing you close to My heart as I pray to My Father on your behalf. Satan is going to stand before My Father and condemn you and hope that He will 'throw you back.' But, that's not going to happen. You're going to fail, but out of that failure you are going to be a different man. Pete, you'll never believe this, but I visualize you helping others in the very area you have messed up. Your past instability will soon become a new found stability. And, Pete, you are going to show others how to do it."

Do you see the value of accepting a family member who has failed miserably? People who accept others like Jesus did are healers and menders. Arrogant, bitter, rejecting people are robbed of ministry and confined to the misery of their own making. Yes, you can get hurt again.

SEPARATE POSITION FROM PERFORMANCE

Separate in your thinking about who the person *is* from what they have *done*. This is much easier said than done. It is appropriate to express disappointment or grief over a wrong behavior. God grieved over Israel's rebellion. Jeremiah, called the weeping prophet, expressed gut-wrenching sorrow over his nation's sin and rebellion (Jer. 9:1). From that same grieving heart he offered to be a part of their healing.

Grief and sorrow over family sin is healthy. It is the best emotional expression for wrong behavior and it is a more godly response than anger, but in expressing the grief over the sin, there must be reassurances of unconditional love and a desire to accept the person back into fellowship. How long do you grieve? It will probably last in varying degrees of intensity until there is a track record of genuine change.

God never confuses who we are and what we have done. For whom the Lord loves, He disciplines (Heb. 12:7). God's love never sets aside His responsibility to discipline. You must do so with your children. You may have to do this with your wayward mate. Some call it, "tough love." I prefer to call it, "responsible love." However, withdrawing your love is never an appropriate form of punishment. God never withdraws His love under any circumstance (Romans 8:35-39). It will be hard but you must separate the child's or mate's position from their behavior.

AVOID OVER-COMPENSATION THROUGH THE FAMILY

Another source of anger that robs the family of its peace is using someone else to make up for your own failures. Nothing breeds the fear of rejection more than being given the responsibility to make up for someone else's past failures, shortcomings, lack of achievement or unfulfilled dreams. A wife may push her husband into over involvement with the kids' activities because her father never came to her school activities. A dad may push his son into every seasonal sport and insist he be the best in it. Perhaps he does this because his dad died when he was a kid, pushing him into the work force early, virtually missing his own childhood. Adults tend to overcompensate through their kids for their own losses in childhood.

Recently I read in a news item that some parents were now barred from their kids little league games until they successfully passed a course in anger management. When the son was up to bat, mom was up to bat. If the umpire made a close call on her son, he made a close call on her and she would go ballistic. The emotional enmeshment in sports is now reaching serious proportions. Her son was not just playing a sport, his mom was playing the sport vicariously through him.

The coach of a girls' basketball team at a Christian school recently told me of an event that involved one of his players. Before a game one of the sixth grade players went up to her mom in the bleachers and offered her fifty cents if she would not yell criticisms and embarrass her during the game.

Michelle's friend, Brian, dropped out of football and baseball even though he was good at them because the coaching staff made it all about winning at any cost and not about the love of the sport. This is not a kid issue; it is an adult issue.

Believers who maintain they have a vibrant relationship with Jesus Christ still pressure family members to perform, produce and achieve to make up for their own feelings of failure or inadequacy. A pastor recently expressed his burden for the way the men in his church were taking on second jobs or ones that required extensive traveling because their wives wanted bigger, nicer homes and cars than their budgets allowed.

Husbands put inordinate pressure on their wives to be gourmet cooks, immaculate housekeepers, volunteers in highly visible charities, leaders in Bible studies and chauffeurs for each child's activities, all the while being a passionate lover at night. Public image is everything. Under all of this is a seething anger that ultimately erupts, spewing destruction at every turn. The anger reveals the need to shift from performance-based acceptance, resulting in rejection, to unconditional love that mirrors Christ's acceptance for us

Education seems to be the easiest place to push a child to achieve to increase the family's prestige. Suicide continues to remain the number one killer among college students. The fear of failing or not making the grades is so frightful that a student would rather die than feel the pain of family rejection.

Eating disorders are as commonplace in the Christian community now as anywhere else. Christian eating disorder facilities are a growing industry around the country. Each bulimic or anorexic counselee I've met could trace one of her contributing factors to a dominating parent who used performance-based parenting skills. Deep-seated anger and feelings of shame were the core of the disorder.

BALANCE PUBLIC AND PRIVATE PRAISE

Praising a person in public when it is not done in private is resented as insincere and is a recurring source of anger. I introduced Pastor Clay in my book, *I Should Forgive, But....* While working through some past hurtful issues he shared with me, "You know, Chuck, one thing my dad did that really bugged me? Anytime I was with him around any of his buddies, he would brag all about me. But when we were alone all I heard was criticism and that I was not going to amount to anything. And going into the ministry was the worst thing he thought I could do. No money, no future." It became perfectly clear that the public bragging sessions were for his dad's benefit and not for Clay's. Clay forgave his dad. Years later his dad finally expressed pleasure over the fact that Clay was in the ministry.

Wives who are lavished with praise publicly but criticized and demeaned privately seethe with anger underneath. Public praise and private put-downs, however, breed simmering anger, a loss of respect and distance.

EVALUATE YOUR OWN SOURCE OF VALUE

God never expected you to find your true value or identity through any other means than from your personal relationship with Jesus Christ (Gal. 2:20). Failure to find your value in Christ will result in looking to people, places and things for your value.

The soccer mom or little league dad who receives his or her value and identity through these means, sows deep anger in the kids who feel used. Only Jesus should be responsible for your value and worth. Spouses, family and things are poor substitutes.

The Apostle Paul had it all and called it rubbish in comparison to his relationship to Jesus Christ (Phil. 3:8). Power, prestige and positions are cheap substitutes for a genuine relationship with the Creator God of the universe. Using your spouse or children to give you value will only increase performance-based acceptance, insecurity and turbulent anger in the family.

A simple solution is possible. If you have looked to people, places and things for your identity and security, confess that to God. He will forgive you. Affirm in your heart before God that you are now making Him your ultimate source of security, acceptance and identity. Then go back to your husband, wife, son or daughter and confess your sin of using them to compensate for your own failures and inadequacy. Affirm that from now on they can count on receiving the gift of acceptance, favor and value based on your unconditional love for *them*, not their performance.

Determine in your heart to role-model Christ-like acceptance before them. Admit it when you slip up and return to your selfish ways. Repent, confess and then, rejoice in your fresh start. Then do your family a favor - encourage them to place *their* total identity in Christ, not in their own performance, achievements and accomplishments. Help them to distinguish between who they are (identity) and what they do (accomplishments). Reinforce to them that the acquisition of fame and fortune never changes anything that is important. That's the easy part. But realize that the loss of fame and fortune also never changes anything that is important either. That's the hard part. Unconditional love and acceptance is what is important. This is guaranteed to increase God's peace in your home.

ANGER REDUCTION KEYS

1. Honestly acknowledge what rejection is.
2. Restore your home as a rejection-proof place to live.
3. Determine to accept others on the same basis Christ did.
4. Stop pressuring others to achieve to make you look good.
5. Replace every negative habit with a positive one.
6. Grant acceptance as a daily gift.
7. Reward positive behavior patterns.
8. Affirm your acceptance in the midst of others' failures.
9. Visualize the benefits of a corrected failure.
10. Separate position in the family from performance as a family member.
11. Stop using family members to compensate for your shortcomings.
12. Establish your personal value in your relationship with Jesus Christ.

SMALL GROUP DISCUSSION QUESTIONS

1. Honestly share your most difficult time of experiencing rejection. What long term effects did it have on you? What are some healthy ways you have found to work through it?

2. How did you come to realize that your foundation for acceptance is in Christ? In what ways was it tested through the years?

3. Who has been the hardest fellow believer you have had to accept? How did you come to accept him/her? What did you learn through the process?

4. What experience have you had with acceptance that is based on performance? What were the feelings you struggled with? How did you deal with them?

5. Describe a time when someone fully accepted you and you knew you did not deserve it? How did you respond? What did you learn through it?

6. Describe the most difficult time you had separating a person's position from his or her poor performance or difficult personality? What was that person's response to you?

7. Describe how you felt when someone praised you publicly for his/her own benefit?

8. In what ways would your family look different if each member accepted one another as Christ has accepted us?

9. How did you establish your own personal value in Jesus Christ? What scripture was meaningful to you in your journey? In what ways do you struggle to live out this reality day to day?

CHAPTER 7

CRITICISM, THE LAUNCHING PAD OF ANGER

HAROLD DID NOT want to be here. As he sat on my dark blue couch, he squirmed. I sat across from the coffee table. The church elder, Bryan, sat nervously next to me.

A few weeks before this meeting Bryan had called me on behalf of his church. He explained that two long-standing members in his church, Harold and his wife, were about to be asked to leave. Why? For the past 22 years Harold maintained a severely critical attitude toward past and present pastors, staff, programs, music, missions and almost any style of worship except what he liked. The current pastors and staff had had it with Harold.

Harold's most recent complaints seemed to be lodged against the preaching, worship style and music. Harold requested a meeting with the elders. The elders clarified beforehand that if any of his criticism was related to the church staff, he would have to meet with them first, a procedure described in Matt.18:15-17. If there were any non-staff issues, the elder board would address them. At the first meeting Harold read his letter. It virtually shredded the preaching pastor and other staff, in violation of the agreement. The elders received his letter and told Harold they would respond to him in writing.

The response was not what he expected. The elders pinpointed the one thing that seemed to characterize Harold's entire tenure at the church - his critical attitude. Then they dropped the bombshell. If he did not take the necessary steps to correct his critical attitude he would be asked to leave the church. One stipulation for him staying was that he would have to get some counseling from me but I had informed Bryan that an elder must come with Harold and make the church's position clear to me in Harold's presence. The church asked me to focus on his critical attitude and not the church issues.

I only had an hour. Bryan clarified the church's position regarding Harold. I turned to Bryan and asked if he personally believed that Harold had a critical attitude. He assured me from his perspective he did. I turned to Harold and asked if he felt like he did. He paused. Initially looking at the floor, this six-foot two, two hundred and forty-pound man glanced up and meekly said, "Yes."

Almost everyone who had to deal with Harold was unhappy with him. At home his wife had become the proverbial door-mat and his kids had just "checked out" emotionally. How could God's peace be brought into a home defined as Christian but best described as critical?

ANATOMY OF CRITICISM

Criticism per se is not wrong. True, elements of criticism can be twisted resulting in a negative experience for anyone. However, the four basic elements that make up the function we call criticism are not bad but any one of them can be misused and can cause a great deal of anger and bitterness in relationships. Harold went through each of these steps whether he realized it or not. Here are the four basic elements of the process of criticism:

- Observing
- Processing

- Concluding
- Delivering

OBSERVATION

The moment Harold opened his eyes in the morning he began to drink in literally everything that took place around him. That in itself is not wrong! God designed our brains to absorb information through our five senses. Observation was not Harold's problem. He misused his quality of alertness. He focused on every flaw he could find in people, places and things. He was looking for evidence of failure in everything and everyone except himself.

It is an axiom of life that your energy will follow your focus. If your focus is negative it will look for flaws, problems and proof that life is essentially bad. It is equally true you will create what you want to see and what you expect to see. Because Harold's primary focus was negative he looked for and created negative results both at home and at church.

Harold claimed to be a realist. This, however, was a cover-up for his self-protection. He knew life was hard; things don't always work out and he did not want to set himself up for any more disappointment.

No one was more of a realist and painfully aware of disappointment than Jesus. He knew in advance when, where and how his disciples would fail, like Peter. Notice how Jesus handled Peter's classic failure, "Simon, Simon! Indeed, Satan has asked for you that he may sift you as wheat. But I have prayed for you that your faith should not fail. And when you have returned to Me (after failing), strengthen your brothers" (Luke 22:31-32). He visualized success in the midst of failure.

Jesus committed the future of His kingdom to flawed people. Yet, there will be people from every tribe, tongue and nation around His throne because of the faith of His flawed followers.

Everyone in your life will disappoint you at some time. It is going to happen! You can choose to be on the lookout for evidence of that eventual failure or choose to focus on the good and be mature enough to forgive the bad.

PROCESSING

We evaluate everything through a mental grid that distinguishes between good and bad, right and wrong, appropriate and inappropriate, healthy and unhealthy, helpful and destructive. Then we separate them as if we were grading tomatoes on a conveyer belt. If the task is to pull off the less desirable tomatoes we will only look for those and pick off the ones that do not make the grade. Likewise our minds are always observing and evaluating people, places and things. The word "criticism" is rooted in the word "critic." A critic or evaluator must have a standard by which to make a conclusion. Where does that standard come from?

Harold grew up in a very conservative church worship environment. For him that standard was normal. Anything that deviated from that norm was wrong. A contemporary worship service was totally unacceptable to him and those who led it were also wrong and should be censored.

The picture in Harold's mind of what a Bible church should be like did not match what he saw in *his* church. That still was not Harold's primary problem. Many fine believers agree to disagree and do it amiably. Unfortunately the third step of the criticism process can be the launching pad of anger. For Harold it was his conclusion based on his processing that began to get him into trouble.

CONCLUSION

Harold set up his own unique standards for church life and in the process came up with many unacceptable conclusions. First, he concluded that the pastor's preaching was shallow because he preached topically rather than verse-by-verse. To Harold, topical preaching seemed to skirt hard issues and appeared to be more need-based than scripture-based.

Harold also concluded that the music was not spiritual, therefore, those who led it were not being led by God. Instead of singing from hymnals, the worshipers were singing praise songs and choruses projected on a large screen. Harold came to the conclusion that the pastor was not preaching the gospel, the worship leader was entertaining and not ministering and the elders were compromising. Thus, God had to remove His blessing from the church.

Even at that point Harold was still well within his right to his opinion. We may disagree with his conclusions but he was still free to have his opinions. It was not his verdict that got Harold in trouble but the *delivery* of his conclusions. Here he exposed his angry heart. Anger not only reveals the hurtful words we say and the actions we display but also the attitudes we convey.

DELIVERING THE VERDICT

Any time Harold approached the elders, he was angry. This was not just a recently displayed emotion. He had a long history of angry interaction. He used anger to change and control people. When he shared his conclusions he failed to see anything right or good in the staff, programs, outreach or facilities of the church. There was a total lack of balance between negative and positive. It was this one component of imbalance that caught the attention of the elders. In Harold's eyes nothing was ever right. Everything and everyone was always wrong.

Harold was characterized as a chronic fault-finder. He seemed to always be ready to detect trivial faults or to take exception on the slightest grounds. He had a habit of raising petty objections to any plan or program. This was devastating to harmony in the church and in the home.

Historically, the church leadership had failed Harold and his family years before. They did not see his anger as a notifier of past hurt. Instead of getting him appropriate help for his anger, they allowed his unacceptable behavior to continue with no consequences. I do understand why they did; he was strong, intimidating, vocal and feared. But eventually the obvious had to be faced.

HAROLD'S HISTORY OF HURT

In my office that day we began to trace Harold's history of anger. I inquired if he had experienced this anger all the years he attended this church. Yes. Had it been there before he began to attend? Yes. Had it been there before he was married? Again, yes. That answer just eliminated anyone in his home or church as the original source of his critical spirit. All those years Harold's anger had been attempting to notify him how deeply he had been hurt by an angry, critical, shame-based father. His father seriously distorted Harold's thinking grid, programming him to inject his father's shame into others through criticism. But there is a way to correct and replace criticism that can change the atmosphere in relationships!

PRAISE IS SCRIPTURAL

What a terrific encouragement the message was to me that Sunday. I could hardly wait to thank our guest speaker for the fabulous job he did. I patiently waited in the reception line. I was next. As I approached him, I extended my hand, enthusiastically expressing my deep appreciation for his message. I no more got out two sentences of grateful appreciation than he interrupted me, "Don't praise me. It was Jesus," as he pointed his index finger into the air.

I smiled faintly and walked away. Jesus? I thought his name was Lloyd. Yes, I knew what he was saying. What I experienced that night was God's Spirit working in Lloyd's imperfect life to bless me. However, as I have observed this, "It was Jesus" response I have noticed that those who state this are uncomfortable with appropriate praise. Usually it does not reflect humility but a feeble attempt to cover embarrassment from appropriate praise.

Praise of one another is scriptural. "Let another praise you and not your own mouth; a stranger, and not your own lips" (Prov. 27:2). It may come as a pleasant surprise to most believers that after the judgment of our actions and motives, "Each man's praise will come to him from God" (I Cor. 4:5). Appropriate praise can be one of the best sources of bonding we may have in our relational arsenal. To acknowledge a job well done by a spouse or child actually emits a pleasurable sensation in the brain to the recipient. Praise is dynamite in the life of the receiver, as much as harsh criticism is devastating. I have watched grown men, successful in their careers, sob convulsively because they never heard their dads say, "Good job," "That-a-boy," or "I'm proud of you."

We are who we are today largely because of the words that were said or not said to us. Hypercritical words stripped us of our confidence. Absent words of love and encouragement left us doubting our worth or value. What a different world it would be if there was more appropriate praise. Better yet, how much less anger, disrespect and rebellion would be experienced in the Christian home if praise replaced criticism?

Dr. James Dobson has well observed that a parent who is sarcastic and biting in his criticism cannot expect to receive genuine respect in return. His children might fear him enough to conceal their contempt but revenge will often be sought in adolescence or when they reach the safety of adulthood (p. 26). So how do you praise someone for an incomplete job or with few positive qualities?

PIE PRAISE

I recall walking into our daughter's room after she was asked to straighten it up. Both daughters kept their rooms reasonably straight. This time I immediately noticed her bed was made. Then I spotted some socks on the floor, jogging pants sticking out from under the bed and a moldy empty glass of milk on her dresser.

Most parents in the observation phase of criticism instantly notice what's out of place. But what about the part of the room that looks great? What is a wise parent to do? May I suggest *pie praise?*

When I was a younger boy coming home from school, I would be allured by the cinnamon aroma of my mother's apple pies. It was futile to try to force a growing boy to wait for that pie until after dinner. I once thought if pies were to be eaten after dinner they should not be made until after dinner. Mom would succumb to my begging and give me a little sliver. I never got the whole piece before dinner. *I got a part of the whole.*

Pie praise allows you to find even a small part of a whole for which you can praise them. Does that mean you have to overlook the rest? Absolutely not. I commented to my daughter what a great job she did on her bed. Then I asked if there was a particular reason she missed the socks, pants and milk glass. I got that "I don't know" look. It is important to ask the question first because it offers an opportunity to clarify the instructions and possible misunderstanding. It also allows you to press for accountability for failure to carry out the instructions. I then reaffirmed the good job she did on the bed and asked her to take care of the other things before she went out to play.

If you're thinking this sounds like a "Leave it to Beaver" house, may I ask you, "What response do you get when you ignore the positives and harp on the negatives?" The *pie praise* approach has a biblical basis illustrated in the Ephesian church.

THE EPHESIAN PIE

The book of Revelation, authored by Christ Himself, contains letters to seven literal churches in Asia Minor (Rev. 1:11). Although each letter is different, they have some remarkable similarities. With few exceptions each letter included a commendation, a rebuke, an exhortation and a promise to those who heard the message and responded favorably.

The church in Ephesus first was praised, then firmly rebuked and again affirmed (Rev. 2:2-6). They received a large piece of *pie praise* for the good they did and the serious nature of their sin was addressed as well.

"Remember from where you have fallen and repent and do the deeds you did at first (Why?) or else I am coming to you and will remove your lampstand (church) out of its place - unless you repent" (Rev. 2:5). This warning spelled out the consequences if they did not change: God would extinguish the light of their witness in the world. It would become ineffective and cease to exist. Sadly enough, the praise and warning were not heeded and after the fifth century both the city of Ephesus and church declined and eventually became uninhabited. Although appropriate praise may not turn a person around, it still has many benefits.

PRAISE REKINDLES OUR SPIRITS

Many of us reach adulthood in a praise vacuum. It was sparingly expressed to us as kids. Some turn bitter and unleash that anger in the family; others become workaholics, perfectionists or praise-driven overachievers. They attempt to compensate in adulthood for what was seriously lacking in childhood.

However, there is an incredible phenomenon that takes place on the inside of the brain and on the outside of the behavior when a person hears sincere praise. It can actually alter the person's entire day. Praise can be one of the strongest motivations known to effect change to mankind. If destructive criticism and perpetual fault-finding dampens the fire of a child's or adult's spirit, then appropriate affirmation and praise ignites the flame of that same spirit. We need to learn how to use appropriate affirmation.

The writer of Hebrews identifies a crucial antidote that can reverse the negative downward spiral of any family. "But encourage one another day after day, as long as it is still called 'today,' lest anyone of you be hardened by the deceitfulness of sin" (NASB Heb. 3:13). Encouragement must be experienced on a daily basis. This cannot be done realistically in the church context unless you go to church every day. The most natural place for daily encouragement is the home. It is reciprocal. Mom affirms dad. Dad praises mom. Sister encourages brother. Dad praises son. Like a ping-pong ball that ricochets everywhere, each member of the family becomes a cheerleader for the other.

If you are the family critic, you have a choice. Keep on the destructive path of criticism or break its grip by confessing it to God as sin and thank Him for His forgiveness. Then go to all the victims of your critical tongue, confess your sin, ask their forgiveness and verbally affirm that starting *now* you are going to be their cheerleader to godliness and success. I promise you, if they do not die of shock, they will melt in grateful appreciation. Your praise will empower them to be what years of criticism and correction could not. Praise ignites the inner flame of confidence.

My wife, Linda, told me one day that she lives to hear my words. I initially thought that was a codependent statement. Then God's spirit reminded me that we do not live by bread alone, but by every word that comes from the mouth of God (Matt. 4:4). Just as God's Word nourishes us spiritually, our positive words are a power surge of encouragement to others. Praise does something else that nothing else can do. It can correct negative inclinations to positive ones.

PRAISE STRAIGHTENS THE NEGATIVE BENT

I once had a friend who publicly declared that he had the gift of criticism. He was a perpetual fault-finder. He became the president of a Christian university. His critical spirit caused the university board to remove him. He had written best-selling books. He had earned a doctorate. He was tall, handsome and a gifted speaker. He had one small problem. His life had a critical bent. Instead of an oak growing straight and tall, he, as a tender sapling, was bent and twisted by his dad who criticized, shamed and devalued him. His dad was a believer who himself had been destructively "bent" by his own father.

My friend's personality was twisted by the harsh winds of his father's cutting, piercing, hurtful words. He grew with a negative focus. To him it was normal - second nature. Is there any way of changing a negative mind set? It will take a stronger force to overcome it. Enter praise. Like a steel cable attached to a tree's upper trunk to straighten it, praise is that positive force to change a negative bent. Praise must be applied daily and consistently.

What could my friend have done to correct his negative programming? First, he could use his anger to identify his father's specific sins. Then, confess his father's sins and turn him and his sin over to the Lord Jesus. That act of forgiveness would cut the negative cables binding him. It does not undo history; it ends his being *controlled* by history. Now he can affix new cables of truth from the Word of God and choose from that day forward to live out the truth of freedom in Christ (John 8:32).

Appropriate praise and affirmation does something else. It *confirms* what God can do through a person.

YOUR PRAISE CONFIRMS GOD'S WORD

Failure is a dreaded monster that lurks around every corner of life. The fear of failure is more frightening than the failure itself. The fear of failure is also a thief of personal confidence. Feelings of inadequacy or lack of personal confidence is second only to that dreaded fear of failure.

Feelings of inadequacy and the fear of failure blunt more steps of faith in men than anything I know. One of the most crucial needs a man or boy has in his life is encouragement, a human cheerleader - someone to believe in him when he scarcely believes in himself. Genuine praise and affirmation accomplishes this very thing.

Dr. Boyd, an anesthesiologist, was topmost in his field and much sought after in his profession. He was an unrecovered perfectionist. The number one emotion that managed his life was fear. Not a fear of failing in his medical career but in his marriage. He had reason to be concerned. His wife was ready to leave this super critic.

Dr. Boyd was raised in a religious home characterized by chronic criticism. His father's constant carping developed the lie in Boyd that he couldn't do anything right and was doomed to fail. There were a lot of areas in which he needed relational coaching. One day I looked him straight in the eye and told him he could be a successful husband and father. His disbelieving look said, "No way." With all the firmness I could muster, I leaned forward and said, "You can do anything God expects of you through Christ who will give you the strength to do it." (Phil. 4:13). His pursed lips said, "Yeah, right." For the balance of the hour I verbally affirmed and genuinely praised him. I reminded him that apparently God gave him the intelligence, discipline and stamina to earn his M.D. with a specialty in anesthesiology. I reminded him that failures do not pass medical exams and state boards. Then in a firm voice with my eyes riveted on him I said, "You are being managed by a lie from hell."

Over the next few weeks we traced the origin of those lies back to his critical father. I had Dr. Boyd confess aloud his father's sin and transfer him and his sin over to the Lord Jesus in forgiveness. Then he named the lies that came out of the cruel criticism, renounced them in Jesus' name and affirmed out loud, "I, Dr. Boyd, can do all things God expects of me as a husband and father through the dynamic power Christ gives me to accomplish it."

When you encourage someone you confirm the reality that God is at work in his life, enabling him to do anything He asks of him. "For it is God who works in you, both to will and to do for His good pleasure" (Phil. 2:13). Criticism, on the other hand, confirms a lie. Since Satan is the father of lies (John 8:44), criticism plays into his game plan to kill, steal and destroy (John 10:10). Your affirmation and praise is a powerful hope and confidence builder in another person's life.

PRAISE DEMONSTRATES GRACE AND MERCY

Grace is granting favor we *do not* deserve. Mercy is withholding punishment that we *do* deserve. God is rich in both grace (Eph.1:7) and mercy. How do we see grace and mercy demonstrated through praise in the family? Let's first see how it works in God's family.

DARK SIDE OF CORINTH

The believers in the fledgling church at Corinth had a lot going for them. They were enriched in their ability to speak of God and understand his ways. Their lives confirmed Christ's presence in them and they lacked no spiritual gift (I Cor. 1:5-6). There were many good things going for that church. That was their light side. They also had a dark side.

There were bitter quarrels, cliques (I Cor. 1:11-12), infighting and jealousy (3:3). If that was not enough, a believer in the church was having sex with his stepmother and no one was doing anything about it (I Cor. 5:1). To add insult to injury, many were suing each other in the law courts (6:1). On top of that they were even getting drunk at the celebration of the Lord's Supper. Some were pigging out and others went home hungry (I Cor. 11:21).

If the divine right of justice was carried out, they should have been killed. Many were (11:30). But here is a classic case of mercy:

God not only withheld the severe punishment they deserved, not only did He *not* rain down fire and brimstone on their heads, but He led the Apostle to *praise* them. Pure grace! He praised them because he heard that they still remained devoted to him and the teachings he presented (I Cor. 11:2). Paul's praise of the Corinthian believers was a classic demonstration of grace (granting undeserved favor toward them) and mercy (withholding punishment that was deserved). Paul illustrated God's grace and mercy in His family, just like He expects you to demonstrate them in your family.

It may seem impossible to find something to praise or affirm in a rebellious adolescent. Have you ever tried saying, "Son, I love you!" or has he seen you break down in tears? Jesus did (Luke 19:41). It could very well be you are the only Jesus this kid is going to see in the foreseeable future.

If your broken heart cries out, "But look at what they have done to themselves and us, too," take a deep breath and slowly let it out. Feel the pain. Then lift your eyes to heaven and quietly ask, "God, is this how badly You feel when I mess up big time? Now I understand what it means to know You and the fellowship of Your suffering" (Phil. 3:10). In humility say, "God, this kid is out of my control. I am helpless! I recognize that if there is going to be a change, You will have to do it. If You want to use me, here I am, broken and useable." Someday your wayward family member may say to someone, if not you, "I saw God in my father's eyes, in his words and his tears. He told me he loved me when I was a mess. Those are words I did not deserve to hear. He wept before me tears I was not worthy to see."

You can be a channel of God's grace and mercy through praise and affirmation. He doesn't ask you to do anything that He doesn't give you the power to accomplish (Phil. 4:13).

PRAISE REFLECTS GOD'S HEART

Jesus is God. He did not become God. He always existed as God (John 1:1-3, 14). He needs nothing. Neither you nor I can add to or take away anything from God. But if God is totally complete and is in need of nothing, how do you explain what happened at the baptism of Jesus? All four of the gospel writers document this incredible event in the life of Jesus (Matt. 3:16-17, Mark 1:9-11, Luke 3:22, John 1:32-34).

Of all the things that the Father could have said from heaven to convince a crowd to follow His Son, He chose two statements, while alluding to Psalm 2:7 and Isaiah 42:1. First, He confirmed their relationship, "You are My Beloved Son." He could have ended it there but the Father did something else. He added the most powerful words that can ever be uttered in any relationship, "In You, I am well pleased." God publicly praised His Son! How many miracles had Jesus performed before this event? None! He was praised just for who He was, not for what He had done. The Father reaffirmed it at the transfiguration before Peter, James and John (Matt. 17:5).

Anger and bitterness can be greatly reduced if you and your family members shift away from criticism and affirm your special relationship to each other, "My son," "My daughter," "My wife," "My husband." Then offer words of praise even if it is *pie praise* for partial accomplishments.

Destructive criticism alienates family members and deprives them of the restorative power of praise, affirmation and personal encouragement. If criticism is the launching pad of anger and bitterness in the family, then praise is the well-lit landing strip for love and acceptance that welcomes God's peace into your home.

ANGER REDUCTION KEYS

1. Identify and forgive those who were critical of you.
2. Confess your critical attitude to God and ask His forgiveness.
3. Confess your critical spirit to those you have offended and ask their forgiveness.
4. Ask yourself four key questions before you criticize:
    *   Do I have the facts straight?
    *   Are my standards of evaluation scriptural?
    *   Are my conclusions accurate?
    *   Is the delivery of my conclusions Christ-like?
5. Encourage appropriate praise.
6. Practice the *pie praise* principle.
7. Use your praise to confirm God's power to work in others' lives.
8. Demonstrate grace and mercy through praise.

SMALL GROUP DISCUSSION QUESTIONS

1. Share your most hurtful experience of being criticized. How did it affect you? What was the person trying to accomplish by it? How could that person have done it differently?

2. Which of the four elements of criticism do you have the most trouble with: observation, processing, conclusion or delivery? What do you need to do differently to correct it?

3. Describe an incident where a word of praise or encouragement meant a great deal to you. How did it affect you? What did you learn from it?

4. How were you able to demonstrate the *pie praise* or how it was done to you? How did you feel? What difference did it make in you?

5. What have you done to curb the practice of criticism in your own life? How did you learn to do it? What has been the result in relationships?

6. How can this group pray for you as you work on reducing your criticism and increasing your praise of others?

CHAPTER 8

SELFISHNESS, THE ROOT OF ANGER

THE UNHAPPY CAMPER

ANOTHER COT SPRING snapped. The borrowed aluminum cot was falling apart. The mosquitoes were returning for dessert. My camping neighbors were watching "I Love Lucy" reruns on their portable TV with the volume just loud enough to sabotage any efforts on my part to get some sleep.

Mud was everywhere. We set up our tent in it. My teenage daughter thought it was the greatest. Linda, my wife, adjusted. I was simmering underneath. I thought I had served my time as a nature boy growing up and later as a youth pastor. At age 55, roughing it for me was not having enough hot water in a four star hotel. Linda looked forward to the weekend. Michelle absolutely couldn't wait. I could, but didn't . . . I was an unhappy camper.

ANGER REVISITED

I was miserable missing the comfort of my own bed, free from blood-sucking mosquitoes! It was anything but a pleasurable experience for me. In fact, the higher my displeasure, the deeper my root of anger grew.

The English word "anger" comes from an old Norse word "*angr.*" It carries the idea of "affliction" or "sorrow." Our word for anger includes the strong emotion-filled passion of displeasure. Anger is further stimulated by any sense of injury, insult or loss. That's precisely why I was an unhappy, angry camper.

Anger cries out for change or correction and relief. Anger erupts when a certain goal gets blocked or thwarted. According to psychologist Dr. David Stoop, "Self-centered anger erupts when I don't get what I want when I want it" (p. 68). And I would add, "The way I want it." I visualized my midlife years traveling the world staying in modestly priced hotels, not muddy tents. Worse yet, the bathroom was located the length of a football field away.

As I listened to the mosquitoes circling my ear ready to dive bomb for another swig of my plasma, I began to ask myself, "*How did I ever get talked into this 'fun-filled' weekend?*" I remembered it was easy to say, "Yes" six months earlier with a foot of snow on the ground. But there was a deeper question, "*Why am I even doing this?*" The answer to that question is the number one key to reducing anger in the family. No, it was not because I was building character, although I'm sure I could have used it. It was something that reflects the epitome of character and is at the heart of every successful relationship. It is called sacrifice, the enemy of selfishness.

ENTER SACRIFICE

If self-centeredness is one fuel that drives anger, then selfless sacrifice is the brake that can slow it down if not stop it. If you think you're in for a guilt trip you may be in for a pleasant surprise. What could reduce my anger and motivate me to go camping every weekend for a month (gulp)? It's hidden in the root meaning of the word sacrifice.

WHAT IS SACRIFICE?

Our English word "*sacrifice*" comes from two Latin words, "*sacred*" - holy, set apart completely to God and the verb "*to make.*" A sacrifice can be anything consecrated to God. It can be something that is very desirable to me that I surrender to God as an act of devotion. It can mean "*to experience the pain of loss or something given up even renounced or destroyed for the benefit of someone I regard as superior; God or even the family.*"

SACRIFICE IS AN ACT OF WORSHIP

You may already know that sacrifice is an act of worship, but did you know that every time you give up something that is valuable to you for someone else, it is an act of worship to God? It's called "worth-ship." You communicate that God or your family is worth the loss. I did not realize that giving up my weekend and work projects to take the family camping was a practical way of expressing my love for the Heavenly Father. I never connected taking my middle school daughter camping as a sacrificial act of worship. I thought it was martyrdom. I thought I was in line for a gold star just for enduring this weekend. It was not until I factored *God* into the equation (mosquitoes and all) that I really got excited about the personal discomfort. "Whether then, you eat or drink or whatever you do, do all to the glory of God" (I Cor. 10:31). That for me meant camping.

King David nailed this concept down beautifully. David was told by the prophet, Gad, what it would take to stop the deadly plague that was devastating Israel. It was David's fault in the first place. He foolishly took a census of his people to boost his pride and self-sufficiency. Seventy thousand people paid the price of

David's sin of pride. Now it would take a special sacrifice offered at the threshing floor owned by Araunah, a citizen of Jerusalem. Why? Because it was at this precise location God stopped His destruction of the city.

Araunah gladly offered the threshing floor, the wood for the altar and the animals for the sacrifice for free. David's response offers a classic insight into the true meaning of sacrifice. "No, but I will surely buy it from you for a price (why?), for I will not offer burnt offerings to the Lord my God which cost me nothing" (II Sam. 24:24).

Selfishness may cost you nothing initially but it will in the long run. Selfishness communicates to those around you that they are of little or no value in your eyes. They are not worthy of your sacrifice. That hurts and spawns anger in the home.

SACRIFICE, THE HEART OF RELATIONSHIPS

Selfishness is usually at the root of most negative uses of anger. On the other hand biblical sacrifice is at the heart of all important meaningful relationships, whether with God, a spouse, a friend, a fellow believer or a family member.

One of the most crucial verses in the New Testament that defines our day-to-day relationship with God utilizes a very unusual word picture. "Therefore, I urge you, brethren, by the mercies of God, to present your bodies a living and holy sacrifice, acceptable to God, which is your spiritual service of worship" (Romans 12:1). A living sacrifice (as opposed to dead), a holy sacrifice (as opposed to defiled). God is not urging you to offer *something* up to Him but *someone*. He is urging you to offer yourself! This was the key to the sacrificial generosity of the Corinthian believers. They first gave themselves to the Lord as living sacrifices. That gave them the freedom to give sacrificially to each other (2 Cor. 8:5).

When God urges you to present your body a living sacrifice (Romans 12:1), He is strongly encouraging you to replace the Old Testament animal sacrifice with something or someone. He is not expecting you to build an altar of stone in your mind, stack it full of wood, climb on top and torch it. But He is urging you to climb on top of this mental altar and instead of torching it, to build a house and live on the altar. What would this look like in real life?

The very first thing would be to reduce your over-inflated value of your own importance (Rom. 12:3). Now you can see clearly how your spiritual gifts fit into the whole body of Christ (Rom. 12:2-8). Further earmarks of a sacrificial lifestyle are spelled out in Romans 12:9-19.

- Love sincerely (v. 9)
- Hate evil (v. 9)
- Focus on the good (v. 9)
- Devote yourselves to each other (v.10)
- Prefer each other in honor (v. 10)
- Be super diligent (v. 11)
- Act excited about spiritual things (v. 12)
- Be ready to serve the Lord (v. 11)
- Be joyfully full of hope (v. 12)
- Endure painful loss (v. 12)
- Always stay in touch through prayer (v. 12)
- Meet the practical needs of believers (v. 13)
- Open your home liberally (v. 13)
- Benefit those who cause pain (v. 14)
- Identify emotionally with others (v. 15)

- Live in harmony (v. 16)
- Deal with your pride (v. 16)
- Befriend the friendless (v.16)
- Admit your knowledge is limited (v. 16)
- Forego revenge (vs. 17, 19)
- Always do the honorable thing (v. 17)
- Be a peacemaker (v. 18)
- Conquer evil with good (v. 19)

Of these 23 characteristics, over half are directly related to people. Can you picture what your home would be like if everyone felt genuinely loved and each one focused on the good instead of harping on the negative? Imagine the feeling one would have if each member of the family was sacrificially devoted to each other and honored each other?

What would it look like if everyone was excited about spiritual things, disciplined themselves to pray, forgive, forego revenge and be joyful in the Lord, identified with each other's pain, strived for harmony, reduced pride and genuinely pursued peace? It would be a taste of heaven here on earth.

Life lived off the altar is painful. A self-absorbed person will fill his heart with his own selfish habits and believe he is right, normal and acceptable, but the end result is the way of death (Prov. 14:12,14). It can be physical, spiritual, emotional or relational death.

Of course you do not have to follow God's plan for building enduring relationships through personal sacrifice. However, failure to sacrificially love your mate and children will cause them to feel they are an intrusion or hindrance in your life. As a result they will feel rejected by you and angry with you. It will only confirm in their minds the lie that they are not wanted. Remember, they already have a deceived heart that lies to them regarding their worth and value (Jer. 17:9).

On the other hand, to link sacrificial actions with a heart of love only confirms to each one that he is deeply loved and genuinely wanted. God did just that. He "demonstrated His own love toward us, in that while we were yet sinners, Christ died for us" (Rom. 5:8). Selfishness and anger fit hand in glove. Sacrifice and peace soar together as eagles.

At the heart of all mutually rewarding relationships is appropriate sacrifice. Relationships cost. What is the cost in marriage? "Husbands, love your wives, just as Christ loved the church and gave himself (sacrifice) up for her" (Eph. 5:25). God gave and we responded to His painful loss. It's not about our love for God but how He loved us and sent His Son to be the atoning sacrifice for our sins (I John 4:10).

Sacrifice extends to your friendships, "Greater love has no one than this, that one lay down his life (sacrifice) for his friends" (John 15:13). The Apostle John also defined how you are to relate to the family of God, "We know love by this, that He laid down His life for us (sacrifice) and we ought to lay down our lives for the brethren" (I John 3:16).

If I had to guess, I would say that some of your thoughts while reading this might be, "Sacrifice! What more can I do? I fight traffic to get to work, then spend my afternoon sitting in the world's largest parking lot, punch-out traffic. That's sacrifice, friend! I put a roof over their heads, clothes on their backs and food in their stomachs. How about music lessons, karate, soccer, gymnastics, basketball, football, roller blading, rock climbing, and ballet?" So where does sacrifice fit in with everyday life? What makes the same thing a sacrifice in the eyes of one person but not another?

SACRIFICE FROM THEIR PERSPECTIVE

It was Thursday morning. My high school freshman daughter, Michelle, left me this note on the breakfast table:

> *Dad,*
>
> *Are you totally exhausted yet? Hope this note coming your way will brighten your day! Thanx so much for staying up last night to read the funnies with me. I'll never grow too old to sit on your lap and read the funnies. Just think! Two days we'll be camping in the great outdoors. Think happy thoughts!!*
>
>

Praying 4 U daily.
Love in Christ,
Bugs
>

Friday came. So did the rain. By the time we arrived at camp the sky had cleared. Friends arrived earlier and were now available to help erect this so-called "no-hassle" tent. Sunday morning came. It was Father's Day. Michelle gave me another card.

> *Dad,*
>
> *What a great way to spend Father's Day - camping in the great outdoors! This really has been a neat experience for me. Thanx.*
>
> *Thank you for being such a wonderful daddy. You always seem to have time for me even when you're busy. Thanx. I've really enjoyed those Sunday funnies reading times, too.*
>
>

I love you lots,
Bugs
>

The funnies? If I was to compile a list of the things that I did with our daughter, wouldn't you think she'd put at the top of the list seeing the Eiffel Tower or climbing the pyramids in Egypt? But what did she pick out as our number *one* activity together? Reading the funnies! A once a week ritual that costs a fraction of any of our trips. What's the deal?

Michelle unknowingly revealed the secret of meaningful sacrifice to me. In order for my sacrificial effort to mean anything to her it must be from her perspective. If I kill myself working fifty or sixty hours a week earning a living and fail to let my growing teenager sit on my lap and read the funnies, as far as she is concerned, it's all a waste.

If I were to pick up our young grandchildren in a limo and treat them to a gourmet dinner and symphony concert, I would have four bored kids on my hands. I get a hundred times more-for-my-money if I take them to their favorite fast food restaurant and then turn them loose on the indoor play equipment. I have spent scores of hours watching them play. They will run up to me and share their excitement about something. I get excited with them. They run off. I could be home doing something that I feel is more productive, but you can't believe how high my stock is with them. From their perspective, I'm sacrificing.

I know parents who are sacrificing financially to put their kids through Christian school and the kids hate it. Remember, in order for it to be a meaningful sacrifice, it must be in an area that is important to them. Am I saying you should not put your kids in Christian school if they do not like it? No, that is not the point. In our family both of our girls went to Christian schools.

I have seen kids who were bitter to the core who attended Christian schools. I've counseled bitter kids who were home schooled. I have also dealt with angry kids who went to public school. The common thread was not the form of education. It was the selfishness and anger in the Christian home. A Christian school is a poor substitute for a Christ-like home nurtured with genuine love and peace.

Psychologist Dr. David Stoop observed in his book, *What's He So Angry About?*, that men who are the happiest and are the most content in their masculine roles today are those whose dads invested a great deal of time and energy in *their* lives. Yes, they were busy dads but they were committed to maintain a positive, nurturing and supportive relationship with their sons (p. 28).

Dr. Stoop points out what happens if this sacrifice is not made. These dads leave their sons a legacy of pain, confusion, frustration, anxiety, fear and certainly anger and bitterness, too. This gnawing void has given rise to a generation of angry men. I would agree with Emmy-Award winning television sports director, David Burchett, "You make time for what is important" (p.202).

Rarely do I fail to read the *Sky Mall Magazine* while on a flight. Each one has the same ad for printed, matted pictures. My favorite picture has the following caption, "A hundred years from now it will not matter what my bank account was, the sort of house I lived in, or the kind of car I drove… but the world may be different because I was important in the life of a child."

Most kids and spouses do not regard a house, clothes, food or car as loving care or sacrifice and neither does God.

LOVE REWRITTEN

Selfish sacrifice is a substitute for love and care today just as it has been for centuries. Often a hurting person will tell me that they know their parents loved them, that they were good parents. Fine, it is not my place to judge them. When I ask them for a Reader's Digest summary of their home life, this is the common description of the dad:

- Cold and reserved
- Not physically or verbally affectionate
- Hard worker
- Watched a lot of TV
- Sportsman; fishing, hunting, etc.
- Critical, opinionated
- Short fuse
- Physically there but not emotionally
- Bossy
- Impatient
- Expected us to do our chores
- Deacon, Sunday School teacher
- Liked by neighbors

If this father were asked if he loved his family, he might wonder why anyone would even question his love. However, God's definition of love clears up any confusion, "If I speak with the tongues of men and of angels, but do not have love, I have become a noisy gong or a clanging symbol" (I Cor. 13:1). So much for preaching and teaching. "If I have the gift of prophecy, and know all mysteries and all knowledge; and if I have all faith so as to remove mountains, but do not have love, I am nothing" (I Cor.13:2). That eliminates spiritual giftedness, great wisdom and "name-it-claim-it" faith. "And if I give all my possessions to feed the poor (or family) and if I surrender my body to be burned, but do not have love, it profits me nothing" (I Cor. 13:3). This so-called sacrifice does not please God. Heroic efforts done without genuine love are worthless and turn to objects of scorn by those who are left behind, empty and lonely. When a woman admitted to me that as a child she secretly wished she was one of her dad's parishioners instead of the pastor's daughter, what expression of love was missing in her home?

From being in ministry over 50 years, I know the heart wrenching demands, the pressures and the expectations. I purposed in my heart to filter significant decisions through three sets of eyes; my wife's and two daughters'. Psychologist and family therapist, Dr. John Friel, affirms that, "the most effective parents are those who have the skill to get behind the eyes of their child, seeing what they see, thinking what they think, feeling what they feel" (p. 29).

Our youngest daughter, Michelle, came home one afternoon and announced that all her high school music performances were to be on Tuesday evenings and the first one was in three weeks. My heart sank. I had just scheduled a ten-week biblical counseling class...on Tuesday evenings. Counseling appointments filled the Tuesday evenings before the ten-week series was to begin. I had to take a deep breath. The brochure was laid out ready for the printer. I'll never forget the inner turmoil trying to decide what to do.

The next day I called the person doing the layout and told them I needed to make a change, a major change. They were understanding. I called my guest speakers who were to give presentations in their areas of specialty. Thankfully they were able to adjust to Thursday evenings. All the counselees were rescheduled. A few people who were going to take the class were not able to and a few others could. Yes, I took a little heat for the change.

My daughter found out what I did and in her "seeking to please" way said, "You didn't need to do that!" That's what she said with her lips, but what I heard from her heart was, *"Thanks, Dad. You made me feel very special. It cost you to support me."*

Dr. Larry Crabb in his book, *The Silence of Adam*, defined the mark of a godly father. He is a man who understands what he means to his children, who is humbled by overwhelming joy over the impact he can make for God and terrified by the damage he can do (p. 149).

Throughout high school Michelle was in every musical and play. The first several years she played only minor roles. To take a whole evening out to see your kid on stage for a brief moment hardly seemed worth the effort but Michelle taught me something about sacrifice. She had to be at every rehearsal including some Saturdays just to be able to do that bit part. In her senior year she was given one of the lead roles in the high school musical. I went every night. But in all honesty the countless hours invested in her life through the years have been personally costly. Sacrifice means to experience the pain of loss for an end that is regarded as superior. It was my goal to support and honor her regardless of the personal cost. I did this because that is what Jesus did for me. He granted me favor (grace) and it cost Him His very life. "For you know the grace of our Lord Jesus Christ, that though He was rich, yet for your sake He became poor, that you, through His poverty (sacrifice), might become rich" (2 Cor. 8:9).

Most importantly, keep in mind that in order for your sacrifice to be meaningful, it must be in an area that is important to your spouse or child.

THINGS DON'T REPLACE LOVE

You may be thinking, "Don't I get any points for providing a home, food, clothes, vacations and a million other things?" Yes! In fact, God explains that if a person does not provide for his family, his faith amounts to nothing and he is worse than an unbeliever (I Tim. 5:8). Fulfilling your responsibility in meeting the needs of your family actually confirms the genuineness of your faith. Yes, it means a lot to a spouse and a child to have physical needs met. I grew up in a home where my father squandered the family paycheck on his alcohol, then abandoned the family leaving all his drinking debts for my mother to pay. She raised three boys on a minimum wage job. At great personal sacrifice, she provided our basic needs.

As important as material things are, they are a poor substitute for a relationship. When things are used to replace or buy love, it causes bitterness or disgust. Men, especially, tend to show love with things. In and of themselves, material possessions are neither good nor bad but they can never replace *you*. One hurt teenager told her mother, "We don't need Dad. We just need his credit cards." Spend *twice* as much time with your mate and kids as you do money and you will reap *triple* the benefits.

A CLEAN HOUSE DOESN'T CUT IT

Kathy is a successful school teacher. She taught high school English to freshmen. What a challenge! But Kathy reached middle age with an emptiness in her emotional love bucket. She was married and had the normal husband-wife struggles. She had three sons who were a handful through the years but her empty bucket was there before marriage and family.

During a prayer time together I asked her to re-feel that emptiness and allow God to take her back to its source. She instantly reached for a tissue on the coffee table. Kathy said she could see a little girl who wanted to help her mother bake cookies but was told to go outside and play because she would just make a mess of things. She and her sister could not sit on the new couch. They might get it dirty. Her mother was obsessed with cleanliness. All the knick-knacks were dusted at least once a week.

For punishment the girls often would have to take each trinket down, dust it and return it carefully.

The carpet was almost worn out, not from foot wear but from the vacuum. Mom was always washing, cleaning, cooking, scrubbing, ironing, fixing, rearranging. She could not sit still for a second. If the girls sat still they were called lazy and would be promptly assigned a chore. Kathy then described her mother's church activities. I was exhausted just listening.

You may think, "*Hey, what's the problem? She was working her fingers to the bone for her husband and kids, wasn't she?*" No, something else was happening. The whirlwind of activity was a cover for something else. Mom had an emotional problem. Mom did not know how to build relationships. She was afraid of them. She used work to avoid relationships and the fear of failure.

No one could fault her mother for a spotless house, immaculate kids or for being a good cook, yet something was missing. Mom never gave herself to Kathy. Kathy could not recall her mother playing one game with her or engaging in any family fun activity together. She rarely inquired of Kathy's feelings. There was very little encouragement; the only expectation was to work harder. "B's" had to be "A's." "A's" had to be "A+'s." Things and the order of things replaced relationships.

If you were to ask Kathy's mother if she loved her two daughters, just the shock of the question might do her in. She could recite a list of things she did but the sad look in Kathy's eyes said it all, "*Mom was there, but not there for me.*" If sharing is the doorway to a relationship, then silence is the padlock on the door.

Kathy's mom did not over-function for the benefit of her family. She did it for someone else, herself. The "I'm doing this for you" excuse was just that, an excuse. Kathy's mother was an unrecovered perfectionist. Perfectionists are motivated *not* by love but by fears: the fear of failure, the fear of making a mistake, the fear of rejection, the fear of abandonment. For her mom, things and the order of things were more important than people.

Kathy's mother had a critical mother. This critical pattern was generational. It was disguised as diligence, thriftiness, discipline and (would you believe?) sacrifice. More adult children are bitter over a lack of meaningful time spent with them than any other hurt. Time equals love, value and worth. I led Kathy in a prayer to forgive her mother for the emotional pain she caused. Then Kathy asked God to fill the relational void in her life with His Holy Spirit. God did not change the history. He healed it and that ended the control of history.

At a dinner party Jesus addressed the struggle between activity and relationship. Martha was thrilled that Jesus accepted the invitation to visit her home. As she labored over the preparations her sister, Mary, sat listening to Jesus' teachings. This really upset Martha, "Lord, do you not care that my sister has left me to do all the serving alone? Then tell her to help me" (Luke 10:40). Jesus went right to the heart of the real issue, "Martha, Martha, you are worried (fearful) and bothered (angry) about so many things (not people). But only a few things are necessary, really only one, for Mary has chosen the good part which shall not be taken away from her" (Luke 10:41-42).

The point is not about shirking household responsibilities but seeing that something else may take precedence from time to time. On this occasion it was more important to spend time with Jesus. On other occasions it may be important to stop and play with children or do something fun with your spouse. Often work is an excuse to avoid developing or maintaining a deep relationship. This may be done out of a sense of inadequacy, fear of failure, rejection or lack of knowledge of how to do it because of never having seen it done.

It is crucial that you honestly distinguish between sacrifice to please yourself that provokes bitterness in others and sacrifice to please others that nurtures love, security and peace. Time spent with your husband, wife, son or daughter in an activity of their choosing is the number one rated sacrifice of all time. Material things don't cut it. Domestic chores just don't cut it.

I asked Helen, one of our volunteer staff members, what her husband does that makes her feel honored and special. She wrote out the following list for me. As I perused it one word stood out: sacrifice. Sacrifice of time and energy.

I FEEL SPECIAL WHEN

My husband makes me feel special and loved:

- When he prays and studies God's Word with me.
- When he affirms me to others in my presence.
- When he tells me how blessed and special he feels to be married to me.
- When he has a desire to know what is going on inside me.
- When he asks or values my opinion.
- When he shares my enthusiasm about a project, a book or an issue that I'm interested in.
- When he attends and is a loyal supporter, spectator at a function that is purely mine.
- When he supervises the children in house cleaning chores on a given day as a surprise.
- When he goes to the grocery store with me just for my company.
- When he values our time together and plans his schedule so he can be with me.

Note her last entry, "When he plans his schedule so he can be with me." More adult children are bitter today over the lack of meaningful time spent with them than any other hurt.

It is refreshing to see a young musician at the top of the music charts decide to retire early to spend *time* with his family, a congressman with a "safe seat" in either the House or Senate leaves the public arena to spend more *time* with his family or an athlete who has many good years left lays it all aside to spend *time* with his family. You are the most significant person in someone's life. You are the *primary* person who can convey worth and value to them. Material things don't cut it. They need you!

Jesus valued time with His Father and His Father with Him. Jesus sent the crowds away and withdrew to a mountain to talk with His Father alone (Matt. 14:23). Sometimes He retreated into the wilderness to spend time with His Father. Jesus also knew the value of time alone with His disciples (Matt. 7:1). The future of Christ's continued ministry depended on investing time with people who were important to Him.

Jesus knew the importance of spending time with children. His disciples, however, felt children should be "seen and not heard." When some children were brought to Jesus so that He might lay His hands on them and pray, the disciples rebuked the parents. But Jesus said, "Let the children alone, and do not hinder them from coming to Me; for the kingdom of heaven belongs to such as these" (Matt. 19:13-14). His disciples perceived it would be a waste of our Lord's time to deal with children. The disciples still didn't get it. Jesus had told them earlier the worth of a child and the serious consequences of causing them to stumble (Matt. 18:1-14). He made it clear that He wanted to spend time with children now as well as in the Kingdom of Heaven.

THE "YES" AND "NO" STRUGGLE

The word "no" is at the heart of sacrificial love. This is not saying "no" to others. That is a different issue. There are times when it is right and healthy to say "no" to certain individuals. This means saying "no" to *myself.*

I was itching to refinish an antique dresser when my grandson burst into the house with the announcement that he was going to play his first basketball game Saturday morning at 8:00 a.m. Writing this I can still feel the same feeling I had then. I took a deep breath, mustered up my excitement and told him, "I wouldn't miss it!"

What was more important? A seven-year-old child or a 90-year-old dresser? If I had promised to help a friend with his drywall that same Saturday I would have told my grandson how disappointed I was to miss his game but that I had a prior commitment. But if that commitment was tee-off time at the golf course I would have to seriously consider saying "no" to my game and "yes" to my grandson. The key word is balance. The scales of sacrificial love should tip in favor of saying "no" to myself and "yes" to others. We do this because that is what Jesus did.

Etched in my mind is the graphic scene in the Garden of Gethsemane where the greatest yes-no struggle *of all time* occurred. Jesus, in agony over a decision that had been made in eternity past, knew He had to go through the most painful death imaginable. As the God-man, He cried out in torment, "Father, if Thou are willing, remove this cup from Me" (Luke 22:42). In my opinion, it was not selfish to ask the Father to allow Him to escape the horror that imminently awaited Him. But the hardest "no" ever to be uttered came when Jesus finally said to His Father, "No (added) yet not my will be done, but yes (added)

Thine be done." Jesus, by saying "no" to Himself and "yes" to His Father offered the greatest sacrifice in all history. God died for man. His sacrifice made peace with the Father possible for us. Likewise, your sacrificial love will open the door for God's peace in your home.

ANGER REDUCTION KEYS

1. Evaluate why you do what you do.
2. Make the mental shift from a habit of selfishness to sacrifice.
3. View your sacrifice as an act of worship to God, not an obligation to your family.
4. Expect to suffer in expressing genuine love.
5. Sacrifice from *their* perspectives.
6. Give yourself first, things second.
7. Ask your family what would be the most important thing you could do with them.
8. Aim to say "no" to selfishness and "yes" to sacrifice.

SMALL GROUP DISCUSSION QUESTIONS

1. How has someone made a sacrifice for you? How did it impact your life?

2. When is it the hardest for you to sacrifice for someone you care about? Describe your struggle. What did you say to yourself to help accomplish it? How was the sacrificial effort received?

3. Describe a situation when you made a genuine sacrificial effort for someone and it was rejected. How did you feel? How did you get through it? What would you tell others who go through a similar experience?

4. How do you respond to the idea of viewing sacrifice as an act of worship? What potential does this concept have to change behavior in your family?

5. What relationship has been the costliest to maintain and why? What motivated you to do it? What have been the benefits of it?

6. From their perspectives, what changes would you have to make to sacrifice for your family?

7. How was selfishness or sacrifice modeled by your parents or guardians? How did it influence you?

8. Describe how you felt when someone gave you *things* instead of a relationship? What could they have done to meet your needs?

9. What do people do for you that make you feel special?

10. What scripture comes to mind when you struggle with saying, "No" to yourself and "Yes" to others' needs?

CHAPTER 9

—⟨⟩—

IMPATIENCE, THE RUSH OF ANGER

It was supper time. All three of us growing boys were stuffing ourselves like there was no tomorrow. I made a boardinghouse reach for the gravy. En route my hand collided with a large glass of milk. Instantly it spilled across the table and splashed up a few feet on the nearby wall.

My mother looked at the milk soaking through her lace tablecloth and streaming down her freshly painted walls. She uttered one statement that has guided my life for more than fifty years. It was not just what she said but what it conveyed. If this statement and all that it implies were adopted in every home, most of the destructive anger in the home would be greatly reduced.

Without batting an eye, raising her voice or flinching for a second, my mother merely said, "I've never seen milk go so far in all my life." Let's talk about why that is so important.

FIRE AWAY

Even in Christian homes milk gets spilled accidently. It's normal. Do you respond with patience or does this sound familiar? "You clumsy ox. Just look at what you've done!" "Look at this mess. If you were not in such a hurry that would have never happened." "Can't you just be careful for once in your life?" "I hope you're happy. You've ruined my meal." "When is it ever going to stop?" "Clean up that mess and no TV tonight."

Variations of this scenario have been described to me numerous times over the years. It is the personification of impatience just "firing away". My mom didn't cry over spilled milk. She didn't even yell. There were good reasons.

SCHOOLED ON THE FARM

Mom was raised on a small forty-acre family farm in eastern Indiana. Grandpa Welch raised eight kids there. Farm life taught Mom lessons that shaped her character and developed in her the quality of patience. The lessons she learned are the very same ones that can reduce turmoil in your family.

NOTHING IS INSTANT

Mom was born in 1910. The industrial revolution was in its early stages. Most work done on the farm, from plowing to milking to raising livestock, all took time. Fields had to be plowed and sown. The corn had to be tasseled. The hogs and cows had to be bred. It was months before the piglets came and the cows calved. Water was pumped by hand and carried in buckets. Stoves had to be stoked before you could cook and bake.

Nothing was instant and everything went through stages. What does that have to do with spilled milk? Without the benefits of psychologist Eric Ericson's description of all of the developmental stages, Mom knew that her sons had to grow through awkward stages of life. She made allowances for the fact that the eye/hand coordination is learned over time. She knew that my hand reached that glass of milk before my mind registered it was there. She was willing to endure the personal pain of the frustration over spilled milk while she waited for us to grow up - because she understood nothing was instant.

GROWTH IS IN STAGES

Mom also made allowances for all the stages of our lives, including our adolescence. Yes, we had chores. By this time my alcoholic father had abandoned the home. Mom had to go to work at minimum wage to support the family. My older brother went to work in the produce department of our local supermarket. I mowed yards. However, with all of the pressure that came to bear on our fractured family, Mom demonstrated incredible patience at each of our developmental transition points.

By contrast, failure to acknowledge and make allowances for the stages of growth in children, could result in a rush of anger that would ultimately explode into devastating consequences. Even the F.B.I. will confirm that most toddler and preschool homicides result from a child's failure to meet the parents' unrealistic developmental expectations.

Adults who fail to understand the reality of these stages verbally lacerate their kids with words like these.

- "You clumsy ox."
- "Oh, *that's* cute."
- "You couldn't walk and chew gum at the same time."
- "Is all of your taste in your mouth?"
- "Can't you see where you're going?"
- "You're not going to wear *that*."
- "When are you going to grow up?"
- "Stop acting your age."

- "Are you all feet?"
- "You've got the shape of a bean pole."
- "Use your brain."
- "Don't you have anything between your ears?"
- "Real men don't cry."
- "Big sissy."
- "Hey, Klutz."

We used to say as kids, "Sticks and stones can break my bones but names will never hurt me." This is a lie. Long after the pain of sticks and stones is gone, the emotional pain of the shaming names reaches into adulthood, even of believers.

Jesus, the perfect God-man, went through developmental stages. How do we know? Dr. Luke recorded a glimpse of this reality twice. After Jesus returned from Egypt to Nazareth with His parents, the gospel writer, Luke explains, "...and the child grew and became strong in spirit, filled with wisdom" (Luke 2:40 NKJV). Returning home from the Temple at age twelve Dr. Luke records, "...and Jesus increased in wisdom and stature, and in favor with God and man" (Luke 2:52 NKJV).

Mom's patience, developed early in life, gave her the ability to deal with our faults, weaknesses, failures and even clumsy spilling of milk. The farm taught her something else.

STAGES ARE THE WAYS OF GOD

As a parent, understand that growth phases are the ways of God. Each child or adult has his own internal clock set by God. To ignore, deny or be impatient with that clock creates a lot of anger. Failure to understand this results in rejection of a child's normal age appropriate behavior.

The Apostle Paul recognized the reality of developmental stages. He knew there was a time for childlike behavior. Referring to himself he said, "When I was a child, I spoke as a child, I understood as a child, I thought as a child" (I Cor. 13:11a). So far, so good. There is no shaming, condemning or mocking of these phases. Then he explained, "but when I became a man, I put away childish things" (I Cor. 13:11b). Note the childish things were put away once and for all (perfect tense verb) as an adult. Again, it was the adult that was to end childlike behavior, not the child.

Much anger exists in Christian homes because impatient adults unrealistically expect their children to behave as adults skipping all the God-designed stages of development. Impatience is not the child's problem, it is the parent's.

God-like patience bears with the pain that children cause through their immaturity and avoids harsh criticism as they grow physically and spiritually. Mom learned on the farm that nothing was instant. Growth came through God-designed stages and everything had to be *nurtured* along for it to grow and mature.

GROWTH TAKES NURTURING

One of the sad results of impatience with children is that it shames and criticizes them for lack of maturity and growth. At the same time it offers nothing in the way of spiritual, emotional or even psychological nurturing. Instead they are shamed into adulthood and though outwardly they function like mature adults, they are wounded and stuck emotionally as children. They struggle with tremendous self-doubt always second guessing themselves.

Excruciating fear of failure also haunts the minds of those who physically grow up but are emotionally frozen as a child inside. I watched a physician friend almost lose his career and family because of constant anger rooted in his fear of failure. His physician dad harshly criticized him for not acting, thinking and responding like a 45-year-old M.D. at age five. Due to his religious father's intolerance for age-appropriate behavior and a total lack of nurturing, my friend grew up physically, academically and professionally but he walks on emotional crutches today.

Another characteristic of an emotionally stuck person is tremendous inferiority. This includes a deep lack of self-worth coupled with feelings of "zero" value. When an immature adult does not calmly wait for growth in a child and fails to nurture growth it sends a clear signal to the child that something is wrong with him. That alleged defect cancels out any intrinsic worth he may have had.

Impatience is not nurturing. It is a form of emotional torture. It results in a rush of anger that spreads like a virus immune to antibiotics. That anger can be reduced by forgiveness through the inner healing of God's Holy Spirit.

LONG RANGE RESULTS

There is something else Mom learned on the farm that prevented her from coming unglued over my spilled milk. Results were always viewed as long range. I saw this firsthand when we would visit the farm in the summer. I watched my relatives rotating from one farm to the other, combining wheat and oats, bailing hay for cattle and straw for bedding. The key was to work hard and store up for the long Midwest winters. Canning was a big deal. Gardens were huge. Everywhere you turned the focus was long range.

Why didn't Mom launch into a tirade over my spilled milk clumsiness? Simple. She knew that someday her boy would become a man. Though he spoke like a child, thought like a child, and spilled milk like a child, in time she knew he would put away his childlike ways. There's the rub; impatient, immature adults cannot tolerate any delays. They do not think in terms of long durations of time. They get deeply disturbed if they encounter any obstacle. They can't calmly wait for a future outcome or result. I have never met an impatient adult who focused on long range results.

Mature parents will see a little man or woman growing inside their children. They will nurture it, develop it and calmly wait for it. They know that in time maturity will come and those children will be leaders in their families, churches and jobs. Becoming a patient person is a process, so spend time on your knees in prayer and live out a consistent godly lifestyle. Never, *never* give up. Wait to see long range results and do so without complaining.

GRIPING NEVER PRODUCED GROWTH

Something else was learned on the farm by my mom that greatly developed her parenting skills. Fussing about the crops or livestock never increased their speed of growth or development. Griping can produce outward compliance but not inner maturity.

I recall as a little boy wanting to plant our own garden in my suburban backyard in southern California. My mom bought me some radish and carrot seeds. I planted a row of each and watered them well. Daily I would examine the dirt to see if anything had sprouted. Impatiently I would dig the seeds up to see if they were growing. I was not raised on a farm. I was clueless about the science of germination. My expectations were totally short range. That is fine if you are a little child learning the ways of nature and growth. It is quite another thing for an impatient adult to demand and expect maturation without the necessary time it takes and then complain about the lack of growth.

Griping, complaining, shaming or belittling never stimulates growth. It stifles emotional growth, produces anger and demonstrates immaturity. Daily praise, encouragement and cherishing words of love and care will stimulate growth in everyone in the family and God's peace can begin to permeate your home.

LOOKS CAN BE DECEIVING

Marlene asked if I would meet with her and her daughter. Marlene was going through a painful divorce that was causing serious conflicts between mother and daughter. As they walked into my office Marlene introduced me to whom I thought was her sixteen-year-old daughter. One problem - she was only twelve. Her height, physical development, tone of voice and general deportment said "sixteen, going on seventeen," but she was entering seventh grade.

It did not take long to see one source of the conflict. Mom expected her daughter to be as mature as her older high school sister rather than a child barely in middle school. Because the child looked older physically her mother expected a higher degree of maturity than the daughter was capable of. Failure to see this can easily wound the child emotionally. Looks can be deceiving.

Or the child may look his age but *act* and *respond* as if he were much older. As a result he is expected to behave in a more mature fashion all the time even when he still wants to behave like the child he is.

Responses to a child who is either more physically or emotionally advanced for his age increase parental expectations. These raised expectations increase the opportunities for the child to be a failure in his or her parents' eyes. This creates an environment for potential anger in the family. Impatience provides the rush of that anger.

PATIENCE IS PAIN MANAGEMENT

You may be wondering what pain has to do with patience. Our English word, "patience," traces its roots to a Latin word, *pate*, "to suffer" or "to endure suffering." It, too, is formed from a word, "to hurt or damage." A person receiving medical treatment is called a patient (sufferer). How is patience a form of suffering? Notice the characteristics of a patient person.

SUFFERS WITHOUT COMPLAINT

When you stand back and observe a fellow believer demonstrating patience, what do you see? One who has developed the ability to endure any hardship or minor inconvenience without complaint. This includes strain from stress.

This person can experience loss, pain or hassle without a negative peep. When you really get down to it he has the ability to refrain from voicing any disapproval, condemnation, complaint, irritation or expressions of being perturbed while really suffering physical or emotional pain. In the extreme there is absolutely no indication of a temper.

Complaining is a negative response to the pain. How often I have budgeted my time so tightly that just one glitch threw a monkey wrench into my whole day. I then experience emotional pain called stress. My natural release of that emotional pain is to gripe and raise my blood pressure. When my pain is released on my wife or children the result is hurt and anger. A mature, patient person still feels the irritation and setback like anyone else. It is no less painful but his pain threshold has been raised by developing endurance from *past* pain.

TOLERATES DELAYS

Living in a fast food world makes little provision for delays. Most of us want it all yesterday. But the second characteristic of patience is the willingness to tolerate delays. A patient person remains unruffled by any obstacle and if you read his lips he may be praising God for it (I Thess. 5:18; Phil. 4:11b).

Often our children are forced to grow up quickly to be the best and the fastest because of our inability to tolerate delay for growth time. It is too painful to endure their present immaturity. In reality our failure to allow for all of the natural stages of life for our kids and mate is more about our immaturity than theirs.

I lost track of the times when our girls, as babies, had messy diapers or spilled something on their nice clothes just before we walked out the door for church. I was the pastor. A pastor has no excuse for being late. He is an example. Pastor's kids never have messy diapers. They never throw up en route to church.

Remember, impatience is not about our kids or spouse. It may be our inability to tolerate the pain of delay. Out of our own emotional pain we create pain in others. That pain results in a deep rush of anger in our family. Patience tolerates delays.

CALMLY AWAIT AN OUTCOME

What prevented my mom from going ballistic over my spilled milk? She had learned to calmly wait for the long-range outcome on the farm. Mom's long-range perspective allowed her to calmly wait as I moved through stages of maturity. Rarely was she impetuous or impulsive.

Mom's patience reflected her Quaker theology. She knew God was ultimately in charge and our time was is in His hands (Psalm 31:15). Her patience was her way of acknowledging God's timing in our lives. What difference can it make if you wait? It can result in a calm, self-controlled tranquility. Remember, patience is the ability to endure both physical and emotional pain including the pain of stress.

ENDURE EMOTIONAL PAIN

I have often asked audiences which is more painful - physical pain or emotional pain. I am unable to recall anyone declaring that physical pain is greater. Emotional pain wins hands down. What seems to send most of us into orbit is the emotional pain from losses, misfortunes, afflictions, testings and trials. When you are able to hold up under the emotional pain from stress, disappointment and loss, that is patience.

PAIN BUILDS PATIENCE

James, the half-brother of Jesus, wrote a letter to fellow Jewish Christians who were scattered to the east in Babylon and Mesopotamia. They experienced excruciating physical suffering and terrible personal loss of families, homes, lands and fortunes. They were minorities. Life was hard.

Everyone who was banished to these strange lands had to build two houses. The first house was a literal building with roof, walls, windows and doors but this was not the house James alluded to in his letter. It was the house of patience built by various trials.

The Greek word for patience is made up of two words; *hupo* means "under" and *meno*, "to abide" under or take up residence, to build a house and live there permanently. Emotional and physical pain can build in you the ability to live in discomfort without any foreseeable relief in sight.

Patience is the house that pain built. It is always under construction. Resisting its efforts in your life only keeps you stuck at your own stages of immaturity. Dr. John Friel believes that people who do not see the value in struggle will be trapped in infancy until they learn to endure it (*The Seven Worst Things*, p.6). In fact, he warns that life will keep tossing the same lesson in front of you until you learn it and then you get to move on to the next lesson (p. 53).

No athlete builds or develops a muscle until it is stretched beyond its normal comfort level. "No pain, no gain." It is one of the ways of God. A patient believer can endure emotional pain because he has stretched his emotional pain threshold to higher, more mature levels.

Endure When Wronged

One of the most difficult patience builders is to endure an undeserved hurt when wronged. A Mennonite pastor friend told me of an Amish church leader who was accused of sexually assaulting a young girl. When confronted with the accusation he merely said, "Is that so?" and nothing more. The church and community totally ostracized him even though there was not enough evidence to support the allegation. Over 25 years later the truth came out. It was not him but someone else. By this time he was a very old man. He was approached and told that he had been totally cleared. Without a change of demeanor he said, "*Is that so?*"

Everything inside of me screamed, "Foul! Unfair! Fight back! Clear your name! Demand an apology!" For him just to stand there and say, "*Is that so?*" seemed totally unacceptable - even weak. Not long after that I read Peter's instruction on how to respond when suffering emotional and in some cases, physical pain. He selected servants, one of the lowest and most despised social positions in Roman society, to illustrate this aspect of patient endurance when wronged.

"Servants, be submissive to your masters with all fear, not only to the good and gentle, but also to the harsh. Why? For this is commendable, if because of conscience toward God one endures grief, suffering wrongfully. For what credit is it if, when you are beaten for your faults, you take it patiently? But when you do good and suffer, if you take it patiently, this is commendable before God" (I Peter 2:19-20 NKJV).

Where do most family fights between spouses or siblings arise? One person does or says a hurtful thing and instantly the normal reaction is to defend, accuse, pout, scream, yell, name-call, hit back and even destroy property. This is not patient endurance. It is angry revenge.

Dads and moms who live in the house of emotional pain are more apt to have a calming influence on all when wronged or provoked. Anger will be greatly reduced as all members restrain themselves from the impulse to retaliate by seeking revenge when wronged. To refrain from demanding what is due takes an incredible amount of emotional maturity that is only humanly possible when God's Holy Spirit is managing your emotions (Gal. 5:22).

DISCONNECT HOT BUTTONS

One evening I was calling on some people who had visited our church the Sunday before. I walked up to the door and rang the doorbell. No answer. We pushed the button again, getting the same response. Not to be easily deterred, I knocked on the door. In a matter of seconds the wife came to the door. "Have you been standing here long?" she asked apologetically. "Oh, I hope you didn't use the doorbell. It doesn't work. It's something in the wiring. I'm sorry." After a few reassuring remarks from us she invited us in to meet her family.

Later as we drove away from the home I said excitedly, "That's it!" "That's it?" my calling buddy inquired. I realized there was another way to demonstrate patience and put away anger in the home.

While he was wondering if I had been in church work too long I explained the word picture. It was simple. If you don't want to hear a doorbell you disconnect the wires. People can push the button all day long but there is no sound inside that would cause you to respond. The biggest problem with angry people in the family is not what is happening around them but rather what is happening inside them.

Hot buttons, like doorbells, are areas in our lives that we have not dealt with from the past or areas in the present we have not matured in. If we are going to disconnect an emotional hot button we have the responsibility to cut off the power that we have given to it. You may say, "I just can't stand it when you kids don't use good table manners." Fine. What is it that ticks you off? Were you unmercifully criticized at home? Hot buttons are usually unprocessed hurts that access old pain. Have you confessed your parents' sin against you to the Lord and forgiven them from the heart? This will cut the wire of that hot button. Then, when your child blows it again, you can calmly and appropriately correct him and give him time to grow up.

BEAR WITH THE WEAK

Impatience with others' weaknesses, faults and failures leads to anger in the family. It is our weaknesses colliding with others' weaknesses that produce the anger.

The New Testament word for weakness is made up of two Greek words that literally means "no strength." A person who is weak has *limited* or *no* strength. His power is partially drained or completely depleted.

This power drain affects at least five areas: the physical, emotional, volitional, mental and spiritual and can create a great deal of anger. We all face weakness at various times and in various ways but that does not necessarily cause impatience, but when we see weaknesses in family members that could create emotional stress (pain) in us, it causes us to act out in anger.

PHYSICAL WEAKNESS

Each family member has his own level of physical stamina. Children tire easily. Snapping at a tired and fussy child is not a child problem; it is an adult problem. It reflects either the adult's lack of understanding or inability to sustain a calm spirit under stress.

Each child will have a different level of physical strength. A strong child can seem to set the strength level expected for all. This can set the others up to be shamed and belittled for not measuring up.

As husbands we often forget that our wives have about 60% of the physical strength that we have. God clearly instructs men to live with their wives in an understanding way, realizing that they are more delicate persons (I Peter 3:7). Wives are never commanded by God to understand men or to make allowances for them physically.

EMOTIONAL WEAKNESS

Betty refused to cry. I would see her begin to well-up with tears then hold them back. I pointedly asked her who shamed her about crying. In a soft tone, dropping her head she said, "Dad." Tears were viewed as a character flaw - immaturity. Her dad's own emotionless life viewed all emotion (except anger) as a character deficiency.

There is a difference between expressing the normal spectrum of emotions and emotional *weakness*. The latter refers to an inability to hold up emotionally under pressure or sustained strain. The person has little or no emotional stamina and just can't cope. On the other hand a person with a normal spectrum of emotions is able to express the full range of emotions in a healthy manner.

Each member of the family is wired differently in the emotional department. One child can be verbally reprimanded and he responds appropriately. For a very sensitive child all you have to do is look at him the wrong way and he bursts into tears. Failure to tailor your parenting and patience accordingly could embitter a child's spirit and poison the family generationally with anger.

God does not command you to merely *acknowledge* their emotional expression but to enter into it, whether it is sadness or joy. "Weep with those who weep. Rejoice with those who rejoice" (Rom. 12:15).

VOLITIONAL WEAKNESS

It is easy to become impatient with one who is weak-willed. They are easily swayed, influenced and impressed. It is hard for them to resist pressure or temptation. They vacillate and are easily subdued. They are often prone to fail. While you may have one child who is as steady as a rock, another is as shifting as the sand.

It is disheartening to see overt failures in self-control. Patience is the last attitude that comes to mind but patience is God's oil to lubricate the relationship with a weak-willed child or mate. You are to "bear with the weaknesses of the weak" (Rom. 15:1).

MENTAL WEAKNESS

Mental weakness is closely related to volitional weakness but can include intelligence deficits as well. Mentally weak people may lack good judgment or discernment. At times they just seem to be simply naive or even foolish. Almost every child has been there. An adult who has built a house of patience - and moved in - has the maturity to be patient with the faults, infirmities, weaknesses and failures of each family member. Often those who cannot tolerate any weakness in others are living in fear of someone discovering a weakness in them.

Our church has one of the largest ministries to people with special needs in our city. Each Sunday 40 to 60 older youth and adults sit together with their leaders. Their intelligence capacities are very limited. I am repeatedly amazed at how the leaders work with these dear believers. They have an incredible ability to endure and deal with the whole range of behaviors.

SPIRITUAL WEAKNESS

Babes in Christ can demonstrate every immature pattern of behavior conceivable. A brief survey of the New Testament letters reveals many relational problems. Almost all of these conflicts among believers are the result of spiritual weakness as reflected by their immaturity. What does the Scripture tell you to do towards them? Here are eight commands from Scripture.

1. Support them (Acts 20:35).
2. Accept them ((Rom. 14:1).
3. Bear with them (Rom. 15:1).
4. Protect them (I Cor. 8:7-12).
5. Identify with them (I Cor. 9:22).
6. Help them (I Thess. 5:14).
7. Value them (I Cor. 12:22).
8. Honor them (I Pet. 3:7).

Are there any people who don't deserve to be treated patiently? In my mind, yes I think so. In God's mind, no. He treasures all people. The Apostle Paul firmly stated that you and I must "be patient with all" (I Thess. 5:14). God will use them to raise our emotional pain threshold called patience. We will become mature, confident and lack nothing (James 1:4).

Today tornadoes have taken away the old barn, hog and chicken houses and tractor shed on Mom's old homestead in rural Indiana. Only the farm house remains. Everything that taught her patience is gone but her lessons live on in me. For over 50 years I have repeated Mom's one liner scores of times with my own kids, grand kids and dinner guests. Whether in a nice restaurant or fast food place, when the inevitable spill comes I can feel ok about it. I can still hear in my mind Mom's words, "I've never seen milk go so far in all my life."

ANGER REDUCTION KEYS

1. Remember growth is not instant.
2. Allow for growth at every stage of life.
3. Forgive your parents for their impatient parenting.
4. Ask forgiveness for your impatient parenting.
5. Start nurturing and stop complaining.
6. Look for long-range results, not immediate.
7. Cooperate with the pain that builds your patience.
8. Expect delays in your life.
9. Endure the pain when wronged.
10. Disconnect your hot buttons.
11. Bear with those who are not as strong as you.

SMALL GROUP DISCUSSION QUESTIONS

1. Share a difficult time when someone was impatient with you. Why did they have a low pain threshold?

2. When are you the most impatient? What do you think is the source of it? What steps have you taken to grow in that area?

3. At what age was it easiest to be patient with others? Why?

4. Share one of the most significant occasions God used to develop patience in you.

5. When did you feel the most nurtured in life? How did the person nurture you? How have you suffered by not being nurtured?

6. Where do you feel emotionally stuck as an adult? How did it happen? What needs to take place to get you unstuck?

7. What ways can you recommend to deal with delays in life?

8. Share a time when you were wrongfully hurt by someone. How did it affect you? What did you do to work it out? What scripture helped you to do so? What part did another person play in helping you through it?

9. What are some of your hot buttons? How were they created? What do you need to do to disconnect them? When are you going to start?

10. Describe the struggles you have had in accepting someone who was weak in an area. How did you do it? What did you learn through it?

CHAPTER 10

─────── ◯──▷ ───────

DISCIPLINE, FORGED IN ANGER

THE OUTSIDE EVENING temperature was pushing 100° in Los Banos, a small agricultural town in central California. As I stood outside the church reflecting on the eight different Vacation Bible Schools our teenagers had conducted in sprawling migrant camps that day, something very strange happened. Out of the corner of my eye I saw a teenager running full speed past me, pursued by his middle-aged dad, Charlie. As they both sprinted by me Charlie was spewing out threats of soon-to-be-inflicted punishment.

My two key adult leaders looked at me in amazement, then at each other. That dad was our local host missionary coordinator in charge of all our eight Bible school programs.

DISCIPLINE DERAILED

Years later one could see the entrenched anger still deeply embedded in the now young adult son, Mark. He was still in pain from old wounds from his father. But something unnerving was happening. Mark was now acting out the same patterns he learned from his missionary dad, energized by his accumulated anger. As Dr. Harriet Lerner, the author of *The Dance of Anger* explains, "unresolved issues from our past inevitably surface in our current relationships" (p. 36). This would definitely include parenting. For Mark, something got derailed through inappropriate discipline.

It is not the purpose of this chapter to explore every facet of discipline in the family. Our focus will be first to clarify what discipline is, and then identify unhealthy features of discipline that create anger. Finally, we will record practical steps that can be taken to prevent or correct such destructive anger in the family.

DISCIPLINE REDEFINED

The library was about to close. I had just copied a number of pages of dictionary definitions of the word discipline. Something caught my eye in the first line of an old dictionary. As I read it I thought, *"That's it."* That's why so much long-term bitterness is still prevalent in the Christian home due to discipline. The very first definition for discipline in *Webster's New Collegiate Dictionary*, copyrighted in 1916, states that the original definition of discipline, "to instruct," is now obsolete. Incredible! That explains why most discipline today is either ineffective, inappropriate, overdone or in some cases nonexistent. The number one purpose of discipline, to instruct, has been lost.

If Charlie had known that the primary purpose of discipline was to instruct, would he have been chasing his son, Mark, around the church, out of control and enraged? Punishment, not discipline, was on his mind. It is much easier to accept the other dimensions of discipline such as to drill, train, enforce, control, develop, correct, mold, mature, pattern, submit, punish, support and encourage. Used appropriately any of these can be an effective form of discipline but to overlook discipline's original meaning, to instruct," is to totally miss God's goal for it.

DISCIPLESHIP AND DISCIPLINE

Before you dismiss the crucial meaning of the word discipline, "to instruct," consider for a moment the historical development of both words. Our English word, *discipline*, comes from Latin, "to instruct," which is derived from the word for pupil, disciple, learner. When you turn to the New Testament Greek word, it even gets more focused. The Greek word for discipline, *sophronismos*, is from two words which literally mean "saving the mind" or "sound mind." The primary focus is the *brain* not the *behind*. In Greek, discipleship, *paideno*, means "to train or educate children." It comes from the word for child, *pais*, and refers to correction with words, reproof and admonishing.

It is not a stretch to see how discipleship is related to discipline. A disciple is a learner at any age. A child is either a disciple because he is a child or because he is both a child and a follower of Jesus Christ.

THE ANGRY RABBI

I can still see Charlie screaming out threats as he attempted to catch his son, Mark and "discipline" him. If Mark was being discipled, what was he learning from the teacher, his dad? Teacher in Hebrew is "rabbi." Dad, the angry rabbi, was out of control and trying to discipline his son to teach him self-control.

There is a verse in the New Testament that should unnerve every parent who disciplines in anger. The Apostle James explains it this way, "So then, my beloved brethren, let every man be swift to hear, slow to speak and slow to wrath. (Why?) For the wrath of man (or parents) does not produce the righteousness of God" (James 1:19-20). If you object, "I'm disciplining; I'm not discipling." Sorry, they are the same. Discipline is a form of discipleship and the goal of both is righteousness.

Perhaps you are thinking, "Who's talking about righteousness? My kid needs some pain inflicted for what he did." This is true, but what is your goal in inflicting this pain? Do you want to punish? Fine, but what is the ultimate goal of your punishment? "I want him to do what's right, to respect me and obey God." I have some bad news for you. Your anger does not develop godliness in your child. Un-Christ-like behavior in you does not produce Christ-like behavior in your child. You may get outward compliance but not inward Christ-like character. Disciplining in anger may get temporary results and make you feel better but your child will suffer from anger and bitterness. In time he will act out on others what was acted upon him.

Young men raised on a diet of angry discipline become angry controllers like their parents. The parents' emotional wounds now become the adult child's pain. Doctors Hemfelt and Warren observe that behavior problems in a child are at least three generations in the making, from parents to children to grandchildren (p. 68). The adult child inflicts the pain from his parents onto his children who now carry that pain (Exodus 20:5-6). Discipline done in anger can produce at least three negative results.

ANGER STUNTS CHARACTER GROWTH

Appropriate correction is a part of discipleship. When discipline is combined with anger it only embitters the disciple and blocks the intended lesson from penetrating the child's mind. Family therapist, Norman Wright, explains why. Children change under pressure and become "younger" emotionally. Anger instills fear that creates stress and releases hormones that actually interfere with memory and learning. Anger-induced fear short-circuits the brain. That's why a child may respond to your questions with, "I don't know" or "I don't remember" (*The Prehisteric Parent*, p. 156). Anger activates a child's emotions, not their mind and certainly not their conscience. It does the same thing in adults.

God convicts us by the Holy Spirit in our spirit and mind. We sense in our spirit that something is wrong then He reveals to our mind what it is. Strong emotion blocks both the spirit and the mind and hinders both a spiritual and a rational response.

Discipline done in anger stunts growth in Christ-like character. Instead it activates anger and fear that ultimately controls the child into adulthood. Anger produces fear. Fear replaces love instead of love replacing fear (I John 4:18). Fear-managed people rarely grow in faith or in love for others (including their family). Instead they get stuck in people-pleasing and approval-seeking roles. Their consciences do not develop to their potential but the religious trappings are preserved in hypocrisy for the next generation while their anger stunts godly character growth in the present.

ANGER WILL JUSTIFY CONTINUED WRONG BEHAVIOR

Discipline administered in anger motivates a child to justify his wrong behavior. His mind blocks out the intent of the discipline. Instead he sees the parent's inappropriate discipline as equally wrong as his offense. So he reasons, "Why change?" Your anger gives the child an *excuse* to take the focus off his offense and ignore what he needs to change. The child justifies his wrong behavior when discipline is done in anger. There is an even more serious reason not to discipline when anger is in control.

ANGER PRODUCES DESTRUCTION FROM HELL

Raymond struggled with condemning thoughts. He knew they were not the same feelings he had when he had sinned. He could tell the difference between the Holy Spirit's conviction and someone else's condemnation. I asked him how long he had heard these harsh condemning thoughts that shamed and criticized him. "All of my life, I guess." I asked him if he had any sin that he had not confessed, "I'm not perfect, but I do try to keep short accounts with the Lord," came a very sincere reply.

"Has God been revealing to you a particular sin you're engaged in now?"

"Nope," he said, shaking his head side to side.

I asked him to bow his head and pray with me. "Lord, we do not know where these condemning thoughts are coming from. If it would please You, would You show Raymond where they are coming from?"

"All I can see is my dad. I can still see the rage in his eyes, but it didn't seem to be just him. It felt like someone else was talking through my dad. It is weird."

We reviewed the many occasions his dad "lost it" with Raymond. He was led in a prayer of forgiveness for his father's inappropriate discipline and fits of rage. Raymond felt some relief.

Then he dropped the bombshell. "I can still see a pair of evil eyes just staring at me." It was then I knew that there was an evil presence behind those eyes. In prayer I had Raymond affirm his personal relationship with Jesus Christ. Then he was told to hold up the blood of Christ and come against that evil presence and command it to leave in Jesus' name (Rev. 12:11). "They're gone," he exclaimed. Then in the next breath he inquired, "What was that all about?"

I asked Raymond to pick up the Bible on the coffee table and read James 3:6. He began to read, "And the tongue is a fire, a world of iniquity. The tongue is so set among our members that it defiles the whole body, and sets on fire the course of nature; and it is set on fire by hell." The words *iniquity, defile, fire* and *hell* do not paint a pretty picture. But two words deserve notice: "course" and "hell."

The word "course" can literally be translated "the wheel of existence" or "cycles of life." The tongue when viewed as a hub with spokes, starts its destruction from the center out and affects every cycle or phase of life. The word hell in Greek, *gehenna,* is a physical word picture that refers to the Valley of Hinnom just south of Jerusalem with a history of human sacrifice (Jer. 7:31) and a continuously burning refuse dump. It is a figure for the eternal "lake of fire," the ultimate destination for Satan. Hell is his place and he is the evil source of the destructive words. Angry words can inflict damaging curses that influence a child for the rest of his life.

Unintentionally you may allow Satan access through your anger (Eph. 4:27). You can unknowingly permit Satan to use your mouth, body language or tone of voice to issue forth the darkest evil possible. Your discipline done in anger gives Satan entrance to work his havoc in the lives of those you love.

REPLACE ANGER WITH GRIEF

Is there something that works better than anger in discipling? How can you discipline effectively and firmly if you are as "cool as a cucumber"? Before examining that let's review. Discipline is also discipleship. Discipleship is instruction, training in Christian character.

However you discipline, it must reflect love, joy, peace, patience, kindness, goodness, faithfulness, gentleness and self-control (Gal. 5:22, 23). What does the fruit of the Spirit have to do with correcting a mouthy, disrespectful or rebellious kid? We may well ask, how God responds when we act out the same behavior as adults? God makes it clear how He feels when we disobey Him, "and do not grieve the Holy Spirit of God, by whom you were sealed for the day of redemption" (Eph. 4:30).

How do you learn to grieve? You just told your five-year-old son not to play in the street. Guess what? He did it anyway. How do you spank with grief? That's a good question. The son needs to be corrected for this disobedience if he was appropriately warned. You defined the limit, "Don't go out into the street." You warned him. He did it anyway.

But may I make a suggestion? Instead of going into a rage yourself (sin), try first setting him down, looking eye-to-eye and gently telling him how sad you are that he disobeyed. Tell him that you want him to build trust so that he can get further privileges. Affirm your love and sadness, then, out of grief, apply the appropriate discipline. You may be thinking, "Why go through all this hassle? It's unrealistic! Who's got time to sit down and 'grieve'?" If you are just a disciplinarian, you don't have time. Your son or daughter may not be your priority. Things, possessions, places, accomplishments or activities may have a higher priority for you but without a doubt more kids are turned around by consistent love, appropriate limits or boundaries, diligent instruction and firm consequences for wrong behavior than just physical pain inflicted in rage. That form of discipline only reaches the child's emotion but not his conscience. Grief reaches the conscience like nothing else. Make it perfectly clear to the child that you love him and are deeply grieved and saddened by his actions. Drop the level of your voice, stay in control and display appropriate grief.

You are ultimately disciplining the child so he will learn not to grieve God's heart and how to be controlled by His Spirit.

As Dr. Friel has observed, the only way children learn to have internal structure is by starting with external structure (*The Seven Worst Things*, p. 14). I would add that this strengthened internal structure becomes the basis later for Spirit control. Self-control is not automatic at salvation. You have observed born again adults with no self-control although they are indwelt by God's Holy Spirit.

Someday you as a parent re going to be out of the picture. What legacy are you going to leave your children? Will it be natural for them to transfer their obedience over to God as they grow up, motivated by a desire not to grieve the heart of God or will they just fear His anger?

KEEP IT SIMPLE

Something else that causes kids to respond in anger is the reign of rules. Adults themselves bristle at rules. Parents who attempt to enforce scores of minute rules usually do so out of desperation and fear. It reflects extreme rigidity based on fear, not faith. In the children it results in fear and anger.

Dr. John Friel further reminds us that a few basic rules appropriately applied are far more effective than many rules inconsistently enforced (*The Seven Worst Things*, p. 13). More is not better. Friel suggests you institute one change at a time and maintain it consistently and appropriately. Many rules laced with inconsistency steal the peace and stimulate anger.

The opposite of the rule-bound home is the lenient home with little or no structure. This home is building the ship of life with no moral rudder. Why is this done? Many lenient parents overcompensate for the rigidity in their own childhoods that were void of any emotional support or love but the opposite of dysfunctional is functional. The opposite of dysfunctional rigidity is dysfunctional absence of structure. What is functional? In one word it is balance. Balance reflects simplicity.

Jesus illustrated simplicity when asked by the Pharisees, "Teacher, which is the great commandment in the law?" His answer was profoundly simple, "You shall love the Lord your God with all your heart and with all your soul and with all your mind." "This is the great and foremost commandment." Then our Lord went one step further, "The second is like it, you shall love your neighbor as yourself." He then concluded, "On these two commandments depend the whole law and the prophets" (Matt. 22:36-40).

If you were to reduce the entire thirty-nine books of the Old Testament down to two "rules," they would be to love God and love others. On these two "pegs" hang the entire Old Testament. The Apostle Paul summarized the goal of his entire teaching, "Love from a pure heart and a good conscience and a sincere faith" (1 Tim.1:5). He kept it simple.

When our oldest daughter was married I had the privilege to honor her during the ceremony for doing three things. As she grew up we asked her to honor God, honor her parents and honor herself. Every guideline that we issued as parents could be traced to one of those three requests. It was a joy to honor her at her wedding for maintaining those three requests. Our second daughter, Michelle, has the same three guidelines.

While experiencing some travel conflicts in the Puerto Rico airport, Michelle said something that dishonored me. A few minutes later she came back to me on her own and said, "I was wrong for dishonoring you." We hugged and expressed love for each other and went on. Those three simple rules will not work for you if your kids see you dishonoring God, your spouse or your own body. They will only learn internal discipline by being around parents who *have* internal discipline. Another important topic is values.

When researchers explored the major source of respect that college students have toward their parents, an amazing thing surfaced. If parents only paid "lip service" to their own values and their behavior was hypocritical, (inconsistent with their own belief system), their kids had little respect for them. Students who grew up in value-consistent homes had their own clear values and a clear picture of who they were (*The Seven Worst Things*, p. 135). When a student grows up in a lip-service family, he will be confused and muddled about his own values and ultimately declare his parents phonies. This will hurt all concerned and increase the anger as well as deepen the bitterness.

Children, when presented with a choice, will model what they see and not what they are told. Children mimic what they see. That is the reason damaging family patterns, even in so-called religious homes, are passed down generationally even to "the fourth generation". If you make positive changes it will not only benefit your family now but for multiple generations (Exodus 20:5, 6).

A few consistent rules modeled by you greatly reduce anger in the home and restore the peace you deeply desire. There are two important things to keep in mind whether discipling or disciplining.

A TIME FOR EVERYTHING
Solomon revealed a nugget of truth that can greatly reduce anger in the family. "To everything there is a season, a time for every purpose under heaven" (Eccl. 3:1).

Every activity has a proper "time" (specific point of time) and "season" (a duration of time). This is absolutely true in the area of discipline. When you keep foremost in your mind that discipline is discipleship it will clarify for you the various functions that must be done at certain points of time and for a season (durations) of time. Much anger generated out of discipline has violated both the point of time and season of time principle.

A TIME TO DEFINE

Family relationships benefit by clearly defining the rules or boundaries at specific points of time well in advance of a crisis. Parents are the biggest offenders here, not only failing to convey the limits to the children but not agreeing about them beforehand. As elementary as this may sound, we have met with scores of Christian parents of older teens who have never agreed together privately upon any of their methods of discipline. Dad may be strict and Mom overcompensates by being lenient. Mom may be a shame-based perfectionist with nitpicky rules while Dad is laid back with little or no structure in his life.

Many times I have asked parents, "Have you ever privately discussed and defined your child-rearing strategy beforehand such as the rules or limits?" The majority of the time the answer is no. They have fought over rules or limits in a time of crisis or chaos and have felt that *those* were their discussion times. They may have argued about them in front of the kids but never calmly discussed or mutually agreed upon them privately. There must be a specific time when you hammer out these issues. Then it is imperative you support each other on the predetermined forms of correction.

If you cannot accomplish this task together, then meet with your pastor, Christian counselor or friend with experience in this area. There is no shortage of books, training videos or even web sites that can be a resource for you. There will not be peace in your home until the peacemakers are at peace themselves.

When the ground rules are agreed upon by the parents, it is time to share them with the children. You have two choices: define the guidelines in a crisis when no one is listening or define them during a family conference or one on one. It is crucial that your family boundaries be clearly defined in a non-emotionally charged atmosphere. The rules should be few and clearly explained.

When God put Adam and Eve in the Garden of Eden He only placed one tree off limits, not a whole orchard. God knew then what we are coming to understand now, that one rule kept consistently has a profound effect on the whole family system. Soon after creation God clarified responsibilities, defined the limits and warned of the consequences for violating those limits. The first couple understood the limits and the consequences. Eve was able to repeat God's instructions to the serpent, "Of every tree of the garden you may freely eat; but of the tree of the knowledge of good and evil you shall not eat, for in the day that you eat of it you shall surely die" (Gen. 2:16,17). However, understanding does not always translate into obedience. Adam and Eve's later disobedience is a case in point.

God established a pattern which is central to discipleship and discipline, namely provide a season of instruction. Leaving nothing to guesswork, God instructed the parents of Israel, "You shall teach them to your children, speaking of them when you sit in your house, when you walk by the way, when you lie down and when you rise up." Why such an intense training pattern? He explains the benefit, "that your days and the days of your children may be multiplied in the land" (Deut. 11:19-21). This not only benefitted the children but the parents would experience permanent prosperity in their homes as well.

Author and psychologist, Dr. James Dobson, in *Dare to Discipline,* underscores the importance of instruction. "Children need to be taught self-discipline and responsible behavior. They need assistance in learning how to handle the challenges and obligations of living. They must learn the act of self-control. They should be equipped with personal strength needed to meet the demands imposed on them by their school, peer groups and later, adult responsibilities" (p.6).

As the children get older, they need to have input into the discussion of rules. Not that the family is a democracy but it is a place for discipleship. If children are not given the opportunity to discuss the logic behind guidelines, they have a high probability of rebelling against those rules.

Many parents of rebellious teenagers have come for family counseling asking me to fix their kids. Without exception one thing was always absent in the family fights. No one was listening to anyone. Dad was not listening to his daughter, mom constantly interrupted her son and the kids just rolled their eyes and tuned their parents out.

The first thing I do before we have a family conference is define the rules of engagement:

- No yelling/screaming
- No name-calling
- No interrupting
- No blame shifting
- No cussing
- No hitting
- No throwing things

- No eye rolling
- No disrespect
- No issue hopping

"But you just said that rules should be few. Then you tell us to establish all these ground rules." You're right. The basic rule is "mutual honor and respect," but since we are dealing with chronic rule beakers that do not mutually honor and respect each other, you have to spell it out.

The Apostle Paul explained the same principle when he reviewed the need for a detailed law, "But we know that the law is good, if one uses it lawfully, realizing the fact that the law is not for the righteous man, but for those who are lawless and rebellious" (I Tim. 1:8-9). The greater the maturity, the fewer the rules.

You would think it would take months to implement these ground rules and get the family functioning. When they are asked a week later if these rules helped them to communicate better, the response is positive. When some of the rules are violated in the discussion process, I suspend the process and call attention to the violation much like a referee. It is reaffirmed and we carry on.

During these supervised discussions you would hear, "I didn't know you felt like that." Why? Each one had been trying to tell the other something for years. But talking is not listening. The Old Testament Hebrew word for "understanding" literally means "hearing."

All those rules boil down to "mutual honor and respect." Negative rules are a result of a *violation* of mutual honor and respect. It is never right to dishonor or disrespect a parent. The opposite is also true. It is not right to dishonor or disrespect a child, for a child is also an image-bearer of God. You can correct with appropriate discipline and instruct with dignity and respect. Children or teens rarely translate your disrespect *of* them into a respectful attitude *towards* you. Honor and respect are definitely caught, not taught. If respect is demanded it will be brief. If it is earned it will endure.

A Time to Warn

One evening our middle school daughter went to a church sponsored recreation event. I was to pick her up at 9:00 p.m. As I waited in the parking lot many kids and parents came and went *but no* DeeDee. I inquired around and discovered she and some friends went to the mall and were then planning to go to a movie. This was news to me.

I drove to the theater and waited for her and her friends to show up. As they walked into the lobby I met DeeDee and asked her to return to the car with me. She knew she was in "big time" trouble. We drove home in silence. Upon arrival I asked her to go to her room and told her I would be there in a moment. She sat cross-legged with her back against the antique oak headboard. I sat on the edge of the bed. God kept impressing this verse on my mind, "He who answers a matter before he hears it, is a folly and shame to him" (Prov. 18:13).

I slowly asked her if she would tell me why she went to the mall and then to a movie without asking us. For a thirteen-year-old the answer was very logical. She had asked her mother but did not get a definite answer. I found out later her mother wanted to check with me first.

DeeDee took advantage of our failure to respond to her request. It was clear she was still 80% wrong but her parents were at least 20% wrong. Then I said to her, "We are going to make this a learning experience. If your parents fail to clarify a request the answer to that request is automatically 'no'. It is our responsibility to be more precise with you and not leave you hanging. We were wrong. You were wrong in going to the mall and a movie without our permission. Is it clear you are not to do that again and that there will be firm consequences if you do?"

It was imperative that each one's circle of responsibility be made clear. Both children and adults are poor mind readers. This was a time for clarifying, reinforcing and warning. It must be done in a calm atmosphere to be fully understood. Remember, discipline is discipleship. The relief on her face clearly reflected that she was glad it was over. We both understood each other. I hugged her, told her I loved her and that this did not need to be brought up again. Did it ever happen again? No. DeeDee went on later to graduate from high school, honored by the student body at commencement with the outstanding character award.

You may think she pulled one over on us. This is not so. I was familiar with Solomon's counsel that there is a time for everything. This was a time to clarify and warn. This may not work for every child but it ignites anger when there are *not* times of clarification of the family rules and policies and times of evaluating fairness and balance.

Before you discount this in your mind, you may recall that God repeatedly sent His prophets to warn Israel before He brought forth His judgments (Deut. 27:13-36). Though God is just and has to punish sin, He is also full of compassion and mercy (James 5:11).

The first step in discipline is instruction *and* warning. There will inevitably be the need for correction. Depending on the age of the child, it may be appropriate to spank, give a timeout, ground, assign extra chores or remove privileges. It is extremely important for a child to bear the yoke of appropriate discipline and responsibility while he is young (Lam. 3:27-30).

This book is not intended to cover methods of discipline but if you want to reduce anger in the family, reassure each child of your love and reinforce it with physical affection and emotional support. Rules without a relationship will produce rebellion. Make discipleship the focus of your discipline. Replace anger with grief and inconsistency with consistency. Remember, this is not a do-it-yourself assignment. God is waiting for you to admit your inadequacy and turn to Him for wisdom and strength to be your child's number one discipler.

ANGER REDUCTION KEYS

1. Visualize discipline as discipleship.
2. Focus on the goal of Christ-like character and not just pleasing behavior.
3. Never discipline in anger.
4. Forgive those who may have disciplined you in anger.
5. Stop attempting to change or control through anger.
6. Switch from anger to grief when correcting.
7. Make your rules simple, brief and few.
8. Focus on role modeling respect, not demanding it.
9. Balance correction with instruction.
10. Prayerfully consider the feedback your children give you regarding your discipline.

SMALL GROUP DISCUSSION QUESTIONS

1. What do you think was the philosophy behind your parents' discipline of you? How effective was it? How do you wish it had been different and why?

2. How did you feel when you were disciplined or corrected in anger? How could the same goals have been accomplished in a better way?

3. In what ways have you justified your wrong behavior because you were wrongly treated? How did you correct that pattern? What part did God's Word play in that change?

4. Describe occasions when you have witnessed firsthand the presence of evil in someone's anger.

5. What would be the result if you disciplined out of grief and not anger? Describe how hard it would be for you to do.

6. How were rules explained in your family of origin? How were they administered? How fair or reasonable were they? How consistently were they applied?

7. How did your parents develop respect in you?

8. How did your parents attempt to convey their values to you? How have you attempted to convey them to your children? How effective was either approach?

CHAPTER 11

PERFECTIONISM, THE SHAME OF ANGER

STEVE DID NOT want to be in my office. In his opinion, "Mature Christians do not need Christian counselors, only the weak and immature do - especially those who cannot get their act together."

These thoughts only fed Steve's embarrassment. However, the pain was too great to ignore. It was not physical pain. He played college football. He was no pansy. It was the other pain. You couldn't see it but it was there. It was inside and off limits. His wife was about to leave him. She had had it. Occasional grumpiness is one thing but Steve acted like he ate bear meat three times a day and for a bedtime snack.

Steve was more than just grumpy. The only emotion that Steve displayed all day was anger in varying degrees. Every word, thought or action was laced with anger. Steve knew Jesus - not just about Him, not just the Christmas and Easter Jesus. Steve had committed his life to Christ as Lord and Savior.

Steve belonged to a small men's accountability group. They asked hard questions of each other. Each week the guys would ask Steve, "Did you blow it this week?" Steve would hang his head as shame once again engulfed him. "Yeah," came the reluctant confession: It was "instant replay" again.

Counseling was not his idea. It was his wife's. It was counseling or she would be history. Living with a human chain saw ready to tear you to shreds verbally and emotionally was not her idea of marital bliss. It wasn't his either, but Steve felt trapped by his anger.

After probing into his birth family background, the root of Steve's anger burst to the surface like a beach ball just released from under water. It was his dad. His dad was a perfectionist.

CONFUSED AND EXCUSED

Few Christian qualities get confused more than excellence and perfectionism. Many view perfectionism as a positive virtue, confusing it with excellence. Excellence comes from the Greek word "to throw over or beyond." It means to exceed, surpass, to go above and beyond normal efforts. It reflects a sincere desire to give it your best, to go as far as you can to achieve a goal. This is the mark of an Olympian.

Excellence is not driven by the fear of not performing a task perfectly. Fear-based athletes, on the other hand, rarely make it to the Olympics because fear reduces their quality of performance. Athletes who strive for excellence, not perfection, desire to exceed and surpass limits, not just to avoid the fear of failing. That is the reason Olympians are not characterized as perfectionists.

Not only are perfectionists poor athletes, they make poor spouses, parents and friends and tend to make less money. Perfectionism negatively affects one's job performance and significantly impairs interpersonal relationships because perfectionists are primarily motivated by fear. When they don't do something perfectly, guilt, then shame, followed by fear, overwhelms them.

Many believers point to the word "perfect" in scripture to support their view of perfectionism but the primary word, *perfect*, comes from *telos* which means "having reached its end." It refers to a process that leads to an end, completion, fulfillment or maturity. The Apostle Paul described this process in his life, "Not that I have already attained, or am already perfected; but I press on, that I may lay hold of that for which Christ Jesus has also laid hold of me" (Phil. 3:12).

Perfectionism is often viewed as an admirable trait or it is used as an excuse, "Oh, he's just a perfectionist" or "She likes things to be done right." In this sense, right means perfect. It strongly implies that perfectionism is normal and it does not need to be changed, only improved.

It is not the scope of this chapter to deal with the ins and outs of perfectionism. Debi Stack does an excellent job of this in her book, *Martha to the Max (Balanced Living for Perfectionists)*. She addresses both the serious and humorous side of this behavioral pattern.

Perfectionism is a very common source of anger. Dr. Les Carter reports that some of the angriest people we meet are perfectionists for very logical reasons. Since no environment or human is perfect, the perfectionists are doomed to be frustrated. Nothing fits their prescribed position. These extreme idealists have a digitally produced picture in their minds how the world (including their family) should be and they cannot be happy until all expectations are met. They use anger to try to get their expectations met (*The Angry Man,* p. 14).

Only 50 to 84% of us have at least pockets of perfectionism. It's found in every personality type and in both genders. Most relational problems are tainted with aspects of perfectionism.

What concerns us here is how perfectionism in Steve's dad created such a reservoir of anger in his family. First, we are going to look at the attitudes present in Steve's dad that caused so much anger in Steve. Then we will see how his attitudes affected his behavior and how they can be corrected.

ATTITUDES BEHIND PERFECTIONISM

I asked Steve how he knew about the attitudes behind his father's perfectionism that caused him to be angry. He sheepishly confessed, "I'm just like him." Steve was able to describe in detail his and his father's attitudes to a tee. Three basic fears controlled them both - fears of discovery, rejection and abandonment.

FEAR OF DISCOVERY

For Steve, public appearance was everything; the house, car, lawn, clothes, hair had to be just right. There was a reason for it. This outward appearance was a front to prevent others from discovering any flaws in him or his family system. What created the anger? Steve's dad expected his wife and kids to maintain a showroom appearance. If they failed to do so, Dad's fear of someone discovering a flaw came out as anger. His every correction, instruction, even simple conversation, was anger based. The anger was a defense mechanism to mask underlying fear.

The family was given the responsibility to help him convince the church and community that they were the perfect family. They did not dare fail in this assignment. To do so meant the "wrath of God" would fall on them. There was a reason for this fear of discovery. Discovery meant rejection was close behind, either by God, by people or both.

FEAR OF REJECTION

Few emotions are more painful than the fear of rejection. Steve's dad experienced it as a boy. In Steve's heart he vowed it would not happen to him. He logically concluded that if any parishioner, family member or even a neighbor were to discover a flaw they would devalue him, or worse yet, reject him.

Value is everything. Pride is an effort to protect one's value. Pride is a core attitude of the heart for the perfectionist. He will control, manipulate or attempt to change through his anger, anyone who does not cooperate with his pride-based protection plan. When Steve's dad, early in life, experienced painful rejection for even small mistakes, he vowed there would be no mistakes or flaws in him or in his family. He tried to accomplish this through anger. The top two inappropriate uses of anger are to control or to change others.

The deepest core attitude that controlled both Steve and his dad was not the fear of discovery or fear of rejection. The deeper fear was that of abandonment and loneliness.

Fear of Abandonment

Rejection results in separation. As defined earlier the word "reject" means "to throw back." When you throw something back or away, you separate yourself from the object or person.

When Steve and his dad failed to measure up to their fathers' expectations they were severely reprimanded, not only physically but emotionally. Steve's granddad would ignore his father for days to punish him. What did his father do to Steve? He would banish him to his room. Correction always involved an angry reprimand followed by a harshly worded command to go to his room. What was the result? Both father and son learned that you did not mess up. To do so meant separation and loneliness.

Steve and his dad failed to follow Dr. Friel's practical counsel that you don't have to do life perfectly and the path of life will include mistakes (*The Seven Worst Things*, p. 129). Why?

Competent kids come from homes where they are expected to make some mistakes, have fun and be a little confused at times (p. 124).

Steve's children were petrified when he entered the door. He would bark commands in an angry voice to restore the household to a picture perfect condition. Failure to accomplish this meant Dad did not talk to you, coupled with the likelihood that you would be confined to your room if Mom did not intervene. Steve was always on the lookout for anything out of place, not for the benefit of the family but out of his driven fears.

ANGRY MARTYRS

Another attitude that gave Steve a martyr's complex was his "I'm-the-only-one-who- cares" attitude. Steve would go on periodic tirades declaring that he was the only one who cared that things were done right. Everything depended on him. If he was to let up for one moment the house would disintegrate into total chaos. What was the attitude that fed his perspective? Pride.

Steve's pride reflected a childlike perspective that everything depended on him. It was almost an omnipotent feeling. In one sense he was right. No one else in the home was driven by his fear. No one else had to have it perfect. With rare exceptions children do not obsess on things or the order of things unless they have at least one perfectionistic parent. It does not take two, just one.

DAD, THE DIVINE

Both Steve and his dad reflected an attitude that is damaging to a person's spirit. Perfectionists do not strive to be like God. They arrogantly believe they are God. Any association with the human race is anathema. Words like "average" or "normal," if used in reference to them, are fighting words.

At the heart of the perfectionist is the distorted belief that he can be perfect like God. When Steve and his wife set out to buy a car Steve researched it to death. There is nothing wrong with thorough research. Steve honestly believed he could find the perfect car and make the perfect deal. They did buy a car. A year and a half later they had major problems with the car. He discovered later that that year's model had transmission problems. How did Steve respond? He flew into a rage. Why? He literally felt he should have known this car was defective. The only way he could have known was if he was omniscient like God.

The words "should, ought, must" are the bywords of the perfectionist's vocabulary. Steve beat himself up because he should not have bought that car. With new resolve he knew he "must" start the search again for the perfect car.

After he beat himself up the next object of his anger was his family. Steve was angry with himself because he failed to live up to his own idealized standards that were impossible for him or anyone else to live up to. One failure made him feel totally bad.

BLACK AND WHITE ATTITUDES

Why did Steve fear making even the smallest mistake? He knew everyone sins from time to time (Rom. 3:23). He was very aware of the need to confess his sin to experience God's forgiveness (I John 1:9). That was not the problem.

Most believers who admit to a wrong behavior would not immediately jump to the conclusion that they are totally bad or a failure in every area of life. This is what the perfectionist does when he makes a mistake. Steve wrongfully believed that if he made one mistake he was totally worthless. He was an all-or-nothing thinker. He felt he was either totally good or totally bad.

It was bad enough Steve did this to himself. But he also held his family to the same dysfunctional standard. His two young daughters were verbally and sometimes physically corrected with the same intensity for a small infraction as a large one. Why? All infractions were bad, bad, bad!

All-or-nothing thinkers are very hard on themselves and others. This extreme thinking makes no allowance for any negative qualities or the need to grow in grace. The result of this all-or-nothing thinking is ready fuel for the fire of anger.

Anger gets unleashed on a seven-year-old child for not acting like a forty-year-old. Teenagers are expected to have the wisdom of middle-age adults or they are declared dumb, brainless or idiots! Such expectations can drive an adolescent seething with rage and rebellion into the abyss of hopelessness.

EMOTIONAL TWINS: FEAR AND ANGER

What core emotions control a perfectionist? Steve readily recognized anger but the other emotion was not obvious to him. His wife said that she could not stand his constant anger. She and the kids found themselves withdrawing from Steve. Anger is the most visible emotion but the second core attitude is more subtle. I asked Steve what feeling he had, if only for a split second, just before anger kicked in full throttle. His eyes crisscrossed the floor. Then he reluctantly admitted it was fear. "Fear of what?" I pressed. Fear of failure. Fear of not being in control.

That explains why perfectionists can incite so much anger even in Christian homes. One can claim to have a born again experience and a growing relationship with God and still struggle with twin emotions of fear and anger.

We have already alluded to several actions that arise out of the core attitudes of pride, fear and anger. Additional behavioral patterns need to be briefly mentioned also.

PERFECTIONISTIC BEHAVIORS

CONTROLLING

Perfectionists use control as a mask for their fear. They control things like money, opinions, schedules, friends, clothes, choices, conversations, just to name a few. Over-control is a prime source of anger in the family.

Control of people, places and things is Satan's replacement for self-control. Why? Perfectionists are emotionally out of control on the inside so they must hide this reality by being controlling on the outside - not only of others but often of their own outward behavior. The controller's goal is to do whatever it takes to control the environment to prevent minimal loss to them. Being in control prevents them from feeling any emotional pain in the present or re-feeling it from the past.

To the degree he is feeling out of control on the inside, he will need to be in control on the outside. Much of this outward control is accomplished by the use of anger. If someone fails to meet his expectations he rewards that failure with anger. The recipient of this anger gets hurt emotionally and is made to feel like a bad person as well as a failure. If the recipient is a perfectionist himself, the anger expressed to him could lead to self-hatred or depression.

INTOLERANT

Perfectionists cannot stand weakness in themselves or in others. They view weakness as a flaw. People who show any signs of weakness are to be pitied and regarded with disdain. As a result no compassion is shown toward others' weaknesses, physical or emotional.

A wife is shamed for tears. A child is told "toughen up," "be a man," "only sissies cry." More sophisticated insensitivity is dished out in lectures introduced with, "If only you…"

Perfectionists demand high standards with little or no emotional support. Compassionate understanding is scarce. Their disdain for others' weaknesses initially causes hurt that later turns to anger.

CRITICAL

The perfectionist will stay focused on logic and facts to avoid emotions at all cost. He is extra alert to others' imperfections, showing his disapproval through words, attitudes or actions. Little or no credit is given for any part of an accomplishment that is good, only disapproval for the imperfect parts.

At work or at church, people do not want to work with a perfectionist for fear of not measuring up to his expectations and standards. Children of perfectionistic parents often give up and quit trying. They are hurt, angry, frustrated and frequently go to the opposite extreme of the perfectionist's goals. They may even become perfectionists themselves.

INFLEXIBLE

Perfectionists do not like changes in plans. Such changes are frequently met with anger. Usually the family bears the brunt of such anger. The main reason for this inflexibility is a perceived loss of control. Remember that control of people, places and things is a dysfunctional attempt to gain and maintain personal security. Such rigidity is fear-based, not faith-based. Anger is the birth child of this fear and peace then only becomes a distant relative.

This rigid inflexibility reflects itself outwardly as legalism and becomes ritualistic. There is a reason for it. Legalistic convictions help prevent one from getting in touch with feelings of failure, being bad or flawed. The New Testament Pharisees were in reality religious perfectionists who strained out a gnat and swallowed a camel. They majored on minors. They so intently focused on the small details of life they never got around to dealing with the more important matters of life (Matt. 23:23-24).

FRIENDLESS

There is a logical reason perfectionists seldom have many friends. First, they tend to be opinionated and do not like being around those whose opinions differ from theirs. To avoid the imperfections of others the perfectionist withdraws both outwardly and inwardly. Contact with people only heightens the perfectionist's nervousness that he might be discovered with a flaw! He cannot relax. People around him can't either.

Perfectionists often obsessively pursue one issue to the exclusion of others. Balance is non-existent. Usually a single doctrine or a pet issue becomes their sole focus. That is all that can be safely discussed. They make few friends with such a narrow focus.

Perfectionism is motivated by pride and a desire to be self-sufficient. It breeds hurt that simmers in anger and blunts relationships both inside and outside the home. Loneliness in marriage and distancing from children is a result. But how can a perfectionist correct this?

CONFESS THE 'PERFECT' SIN

What is the 'perfect' sin? Perfectionism! It is pure pride with one foot on fear and the other on personal shame. Neither of those are from God. Once you admit them to yourself and confess them to God as sin, you have taken the hardest step (I John 1:9). None of the fruit of the Spirit or the qualities of God are reflected by perfectionism. Pride must be confessed for what it is, sin! It is an admission before God that you began your new life by faith but are now attempting to become perfect through human efforts (Gal. 3:3). The Apostle Paul explains that those who are trapped in this pattern of life have been "bewitched" by the evil one (Gal. 3:1). "Bewitched" means that the person is manipulated or charmed by an evil eye into thinking they can become perfect by human effort. Perfectionism is such an excused trait because it looks so good on the outside but in reality it hides a heart full of pride, self-absorption, void of mercy and compassion (Matt. 23:25-27). But it is all correctable. The first step may be to start with a simple prayer:

> *Dear Heavenly Father, I have come to realize that I have been deceiving myself into living a life of pride, self-absorption and performance-based acceptance. I repent of this pride and now accept your gift of forgiveness. I purpose in my heart to acknowledge my needs and take them to You rather than deny them in pride. Thank You. Amen.*

That was hard but you have just increased the presence of God's peace in your home because His peace now is at home in your heart. Peace at home is in direct proportion to peace in the hearts of those in the home.

Dave Burchett in his book, *When Bad Christians Happen to Good People*, quotes Rebecca Manley Pippert. "God is making us holy. But there is a requirement for learning how to submit to God's authority: humility. We won't get very far in the development of holiness if we are defensive about our flaws. That is why holy people are so easy to be with. They have been around God too long to try to pretend they are perfect. They are the first to acknowledge their pride and their fault" (p. 234).

IDENTIFY THE SOURCE OF SHAME

Shame, in addition to fear, also controls the perfectionist. Ask God's Spirit to direct you to the source of the shame. Was it things you did in the past? Was it things that were done to you (molestation)? Was it something done around you (alcoholic parents)? If the shame came from your sin, confess it to God. Jesus died for both your sin and your shame (Heb.12:2).

First, if it was something done to you, picture yourself standing before the Lord Jesus and the offender standing next to you and then confess aloud their sin against you. Acknowledge the Lord's responsibility to punish them (Rom. 12:19) but ask Him to grant them grace, mercy and pardon just like He granted to you (Eph. 4:32). Now send the offender over to the Lord Jesus and say "goodbye." The word "forgiveness" literally means "to send away." If it was something that was done around you, forgive those who did it, then accept it as part of your past instead of resisting it or denying it.

A friend of mine had a mentally handicapped brother. He was teased and ridiculed about that. The shame was terrible. He felt he had to be perfect to cover up for his brother. He lived in fear that others would discover he had a handicapped brother. He has forgiven those who shamed him. He has fully accepted his brother and now sees the benefit God wanted to give him through his brother.

CONFRONT THE FEAR

The hardest thing for perfectionists may be to admit their fear. Ask God to reveal to you the sources of the fear of rejection and abandonment. Usually it is a critical parent or primary guardian. Bring them to the Lord Jesus in prayer and process it just like you did the shame. This is not a love issue. Confessing your parent's sin against you does not mean you do not love him or he did not love you. All of us have been hurt by those we love.

Honestly identify the historical source of the rejection. Forgive the people who were involved. Share what you fear being discovered about you with someone you have confidence in. Remember, perfectionism is a form of hiding from your fears. I have watched hundreds of people become free of the sinful influence of perfectionism when they can honestly confront their fear and kiss the monster of fear on the nose.

The book of James was directed to believers who came out of Judaism. As practiced in the first century, Judaism was very performance-based. The Pharisees epitomized it. James offers a simple doorway to the freedom we have in Christ. "Confess your sins to one another and pray for one another so that you may be healed" (James 5:16). Appropriately expressing your sins, flaws and shortcomings to others opens the door to prayer and healing.

IDENTIFY THE HUMAN ALTARS

To deal with his perfectionism, Steve first had to identify the human altars in his own heart. I asked Steve whose approval he was attempting to get by his rigorous performance. It was tough to admit. Sheepishly he acknowledged it was his dad who was deceased. Steve described his craving for approval. It was like climbing a ladder of performance. When he reached the top there was always another ladder there to climb. It never ended.

I explained how idol worshipers offered sacrifices on an altar in hopes that their god would grant them favor. I asked him if he was performing for his dad like a worshiper performed for a pagan deity in order to gain his favor. Steve did not like the analogy but he wanted to be free.

The first step toward freedom was to see that his dad had become his God-substitute. It was a form of relational idolatry. God did not leave any guess work about this issue. He clearly stated in the Ten Commandments, "You shall have no other gods before Me" (Ex. 20:3).

Steve finally admitted to himself that his dad was flawed and a sinner just like the rest of us (Rom. 3:23). He understood that his father's weaknesses were a part of his humanity. This was the first step in destroying the human altar of performance-based acceptance.

CONFESS THE IDOLATRY

The second step for Steve was to confess to God the sin of parental idolatry (I John 1:9). It is sin. Jesus declared, "He who loves father or mother more than Me is not worthy of Me" (Matt. 10:37). Most of his decisions were based on how to win his dad's approval instead of what God wanted him to do with his life. The driving need for parental approval is a substitute for being led by God's Spirit.

DESTROY THE ALTAR

Next, I asked Steve to picture in his mind cooperating with God in destroying the altar of parental approval. Then, picture himself climbing up on God's altar to present himself as a living sacrifice (Rom. 12:1-2), not to get God's approval but out of appreciation for the acceptance he received through Christ.

The Apostle Paul was not motivated to serve God out of fear of His rejection. Instead he was constrained by a love for God for all He had already done for him (2 Cor. 5:14). In the Old Testament when pagan altars were destroyed new altars were rebuilt to the true God (Judges 6:25-26). Just to destroy an unholy altar and fail to replace it with a holy one only creates a greater vacuum later to be filled with more performance-based behavior.

Parents whose love is performance-based become their children's God-substitute but since they can never completely please their parents, they get hurt and angry and peace leaves the home. Dr. James Dobson warns, "One of the most serious threats to emotional health occurs when a child faces demands that he cannot satisfy" (p. 198). There is no Godlike peace in a performance-based home either between the parents or between the children and the parents. Performance-based conditional love is *not* from God.

SWITCH ALTARS

To break the control of perfectionism you must choose to transfer the ultimate object of dependence from human idols to God alone. After 45 years of striving to win his father's acceptance, Steve finally laid it aside and relaxed in God's acceptance. It was a major paradigm shift. The Apostle Paul commended the church at Thessalonica for making a similar shift in their lives. He praised them for how they turned *from* idols to serve the living God (I Thess. 1:9). Many of these new Thessalonian believers had been pagan Gentiles. Their entire lives and economic and social structure revolved around pagan temple rituals. Leaving behind all that culture was a shock to their system. They made the switch but not without personal cost (I Thess. 1:6).

Steve did the hard thing. He openly switched his ultimate source of acceptance and approval from his earthly father to his Heavenly Father. Before this Steve believed that only his dad could supply the acceptance he needed. Steve was now able to confidently assert, "My God shall supply all my needs according to His riches in glory in Christ Jesus" (Phil. 4:19). He learned that his Heavenly Father delighted in meeting his needs (Rev. 3:18) in contrast to his totally self-absorbed earthly father.

What happened to Steve's anxiety level? It went from a ten to a zero. Instead of flaring up in anger when things around him seemed cluttered, he gained a balance between perfectionism and normal household orderliness. The gray depression slowly lifted from the home. His unhealthy anger was kept in check. God's peace moved in the day Steve's perfectionism began to move out.

ANGER REDUCTION KEYS

1. Acknowledge any fear that is at the root of your perfectionism.
2. Honestly admit your pride that is masked by perfectionism.
3. Stop supporting your perfectionism with anger.
4. Release your family from the responsibility to create a perfect atmosphere for you.
5. Adjust your unrealistic expectations of yourself and others.
6. Replace outward control of people with inward control by God's Spirit.
7. Honestly confess pride for what it is - sin.
8. Remove the shame that energizes perfectionism.
9. Forgive those who have rejected you.
10. Destroy any altars of performance-based acceptance.
11. Resolve to transfer your ultimate dependence on God.

SMALL GROUP DISCUSSION QUESTIONS

1. What is the difference between perfectionism and excellence? What is the motive of each? How would a believer's life be motivated differently by excellence instead of perfectionism?

2. What has been your personal experience living with or working around a perfectionist? How did it make you feel? How did it influence your life?

3. What perfectionistic tendencies have you observed in yourself? How do you feel they were developed? What emotions are behind them? What influence have they had on your quality of life? What influence has it had on your relationships?

4. What connection have you personally observed between perfectionism and anger?

5. What connection is there between pride and perfectionism and why?

6. How have you attempted to gain approval through performance? How do you feel it was developed in you? What did you do to correct it? What scripture was meaningful to you in this process?

CHAPTER 12

HURTS, A FREQUENT SOURCE OF ANGER

I'VE KNOWN JEFF for years. He was raised in a single parent home by his mother who never married. He attended a private Christian school, excelled in speech and drama, was handsome and talented but he had one small problem. This small problem frequently robbed Jeff and his mother of any peace in their home. Why? Jeff was a rager!

A PLAN FOR PEACE

It is tough for a twenty-year-old to admit to himself, let alone to others, that life is not working for him and that he needs to do something about it. Jeff needed a plan, one that would actually replace his rage with peace. Great, but how?

ANGER - A FRIEND

Jeff grew up in an overly controlling church. One of the unspoken rules was, "Thou shalt not be angry!" What were you to do with the emotion of anger common to everyone, including believers? Simple, just deny it. Good Christians never get angry! Even when Scripture says, "Be angry and yet do not sin" (Eph. 4:26) the church heard, "Do not sin by being angry." This is a biblical rewrite. What happens to stuffed anger? Since no emotion is buried, never to rise again, it accumulates and can grow into full blown rage.

My first comment to Jeff after he revealed his battle with anger was, "Great!" Jeff stared at me wide-eyed. He had heard many sermons on anger including such points as:

1. Anger is the fruit of the flesh (Gal. 5:20).
2. Anger needs to be put away (Eph. 4:31).
3. Anger never produces the righteousness of God (James 1:20).
4. Anger, if not dealt with, will develop into bitterness (Heb. 12:15).
5. Anger and bitterness are very destructive emotions (Heb. 12:15).

These are all true. One small problem, Jeff knew this already. He did not come to me for a sermon on the negative points of anger. He did not want a review. He wanted release.

The very first step is to welcome your anger as a friend and give yourself permission to feel it. I didn't say, "Act it out," I said, "Just feel it!"

Like a red light on the car's dashboard that notifies you of a need, anger is a notifier. When Jeff told me he was full of rage, I said, "Great" as I grabbed my clipboard ready to write. With a voice bordering on the verge of excitement I said, "Let yourself feel the anger, and let the Lord take you back to all those sources of anger." We paused and prayed to that end. Why is it important to *feel* the anger before going to prayer?

- If you do not honestly acknowledge the anger you will not acknowledge the offense.

- If you do not acknowledge the offense you will not acknowledge the offender.
- If you do not acknowledge the offender you will not forgive.
- If you do not forgive you will remain in the bondage of bitterness and rage.

Anger can be a friend if it leads you to the offense and offender so that you can forgive them from the heart. (Matt. 18:35). Acknowledging the anger prepares you for the next step, identify offenses.

IDENTIFY THE OFFENSE

As I looked up from our prayer my eyes met a set of angry eyes. "I think I am most angry at my mom," Jeff confessed in hushed tones expecting sermon 38-C, "Children honor your parents" (Eph. 6:2). The issue here is not a matter of honor. It is what to do with hurt. That is the reason I asked Jeff to share with me how he felt his mother hurt him. He shot back, "I'm not going to blame my mom for my own bad choices and attitudes."

Jeff's statement reflected two important issues that get easily confused, justice and justification. Justifying continued wrong behavior, choices or attitudes because of what someone else did to you is wrong. Claiming you are powerless to change your behavior because of someone else's sin against you is an excuse.

However, justice is another issue. Others' sin against you demands justice. Their sin needs to be paid for. When you can name their offense, transferring them and their sin over to the Lord Jesus Christ, you will recognize that His death on the cross satisfied the need for justice (I John 2:2). This process is now your doorway to freedom.

I explained to Jeff that we're not looking to excuse her sin but to forgive it and escape the trap of rage. He is not his mother's judge (Romans 14:4) but he is responsible to identify and forgive her sin against him just as God in Christ forgave him (Eph. 4:32).

"Yeah, but I love my mom," Jeff blurted out. He did not understand that identifying others' offenses are not a lack of love for them. When you sin against God He still loves you (Rom. 8:31-39). It is a forgiveness and fellowship issue. The Apostle John expressed it this way, "But if we walk in the light as He is in the light, we have fellowship with one another, and the blood of Jesus Christ His Son cleanses us from all sin" (I John 1:7). To gain freedom and peace, yours or others' sins must be clearly named and forgiven.

"Jeff, feel your anger and allow the Lord to lead you to the source of those hurts." With very little coaching Jeff revealed the hurts caused by his mom:

- Forced me to grow up too fast.
- Made me emotionally dependent on her.
- Made me responsible for her emotional well-being.
- Told me what to believe and did not allow me to question her.
- Never allowed me to have an opinion different from hers.
- Made me her husband replacement.
- Was jealous of any potential girlfriend.
- Restricted me from having friends my own age, insisting on being my best friend.
- Never allowed me to have choices.
- Insisted on tagging along wherever I went with my friends.

- Was very controlling because of her fear.
- Lived a hypocritical lifestyle that did not reflect her religious convictions.
- Distorted my view of God, a wife and a mother.
- Insisted on perfection.
- Based acceptance on performance.
- Treated me like a 12 year old at 20.
- Made me responsible to rescue her from her bad decisions.
- Didn't allow me to express normal emotions, like anger.

As his eyes darted back and forth on the beige carpet I asked, "Is there anything else your mother did that hurt you?" I urged him to look thoroughly. "No, that's enough." There is an important reason I asked Jeff that question. The goal is to allow God to do a deep healing. Often your healing is in direct proportion to two things. First, the depth you allow yourself to *access* the pain from the offenses. Second, how thoroughly you *acknowledge* the offenses. You can access the pain, then, quickly deny it just as you can open a book but not read it. God desires to facilitate both forgiveness and emotional healing from the heart (Matt. 18:35). That is a result of both accessing the pain and fully acknowledging its reality.

An important step in bringing God's peace into your home is to honestly name all the offenses as sin. You cannot plea bargain away yours or others' sin. Confession (Greek: *hormolegeo*) literally means, "to speak the same thing." When you confess your sin to God, you are not informing Him of something that escaped His notice. You are agreeing with God about what He already knows you did. You are agreeing or "saying the same thing" He says about your sin.

This holds true when you name others' sin. I had this driven home to me by Polly. Her father molested her as a young child. In her prayer of confession of her father's sin, she merely stated that he "messed" with her.

"He messed with you?" I inquired.

"No, he (she mumbled the next words)."

"Excuse me, I did not hear you."

"He... raped me!" came the shout from the top of her voice as she burst into deep sobs.

A female staff member and I watched Polly released from false shame and enter into new found freedom. This was due in part to her willingness to name the sin and feel the pain. It is not important to describe sin, but it is crucial to name it (I Cor. 6:9-11).

Like Polly, Jeff was able to give himself permission to feel the anger. Next, he asked God to trace the anger back to its root. It was tough but he did it. Now a crucial act of obedience must be taken. There is absolutely no lasting peace in any home without it. God has no substitute for it. Freedom lies just beyond it - the hard work of forgiveness.

UNDERSTANDING IS NOT FORGIVENESS

"But I know why my mom did all this junk. I understand what she has had to struggle with all her life." It is good to understand. It can be helpful in healing to come to an understanding of why people did what they did. However, a very important distinction must be made here. Understanding is _not_ forgiveness. God has understood from eternity past why you sin. He understands your constitution and remembers you are but dust (Psalm 103:14). Or as The Message paraphrases it, "He knows us inside out, keeps in mind that we're made of mud."

Yet, God insists that we "confess our sins," agreeing with Him about what we did. Then God's gracious response is, "He is faithful and just to forgive us our sins and to cleanse us from all unrighteousness" (I John 1:9). It was time for Jeff to follow God's pattern.

FORGIVE THE OFFENDER

As we began to pray, I asked Jeff to picture himself standing before the Lord Jesus. Why Jesus? Because Jesus issued a personal invitation to come to Him, especially if you are tired and worn out with life, religion or difficult relationships (Matt. 11:28-30).

Next, I explained to Jeff that he should confess each of his mother's sins against him to the Lord out loud. I made it clear he was not to plea bargain them away. He was not to minimize, excuse or defend her. It was a time to agree with God concerning what she did. I also suggested he picture his mom standing next to him. Sometimes it is hard to say these things, visualizing the loved one listening, but there is an important reason to do this, as you will see.

I had copied down his list of hurts so I told him I would read aloud each offense. He was to confess her sin against him to the Lord, sharing any other thoughts or feelings with Him that came to mind. At first it was awkward but the further he went down his list I could see the release beginning. I could hear it in his voice. After Jeff went through his list I asked him to go as deeply as possible and ask the Lord if there was any other pain that needed to be confessed (Psalm 139:23-24). After a pause he said, "That's it."

ACKNOWLEDGE REVENGE

Because revenge is God's responsibility, not ours, I had Jeff pray: "Lord, I *acknowledge* it is Your responsibility to exact revenge on my mother for her sin against me (Rom. 12:19). However, because of Your death on the cross as payment for sin (I John 2:2), I ask You to grant my mother grace, mercy and pardon, just like You granted to me" (Matt. 6:9-13).

Then I had Jeff talk about his mother in the prayer and tell her how she had hurt him. He told her it was Jesus' responsibility to punish her, but because of His death on the cross, he had asked God to grant her the same grace, mercy and pardon that he received.

SEND THEM AWAY

Jeff was now encouraged to say to her, "I now send you and your sin over to the Lord Jesus Christ." Why? Because the word forgiveness literally means "to send forth, send away" (Greek: *apo*, from; *hiemi*, to send).

For years I have asked people what action they pictured in their minds when they forgave someone. 95% of the time they say, "Nothing." Now when I ask the same question of those I have led in prayer, they recall the picture of sending both the offender and their sin over to the Lord Jesus.

RECEIVE FORGIVENESS

Jeff had dealt with his mother's sin. Now he needed to face the responsibility for his own anger, bitterness and resentment resulting in rage. I led Jeff in the following prayer:

Dear Heavenly Father, I confess to you the sinful response of my anger, my bitterness and the many times I demonstrated it in rage. I ask you to forgive me for my sin (I John 1:9). I also take back all the ground, opportunity and energy that I have given over to Satan in my life (Eph. 4:27). I now purpose in my heart to use it for Your honor and glory (I Cor. 6:30), for my family and friends (Gal. 6:10) and a better quality of life for myself.

ACCEPT THE LOSS

In my opinion the next step is the hardest part of forgiveness, to accept the loss and pain inflicted by others. You will live with the loss either in bitterness or forgiveness. The choice is yours. Jeff chose to pray the following prayer:

I acknowledge I cannot undo history. But I now accept upon myself the consequences of my mother's sin against me. I purpose in my heart to take every one of those consequences and convert them into a positive benefit for Your honor and glory, for my family and friends and a better quality of life for myself (Gen. 45:5; 50:20). As an act of my will I even thank you for those things (I Thess. 5:18) and for what you are going to do through them in my life (2 Cor. 1:6-77).

Jeff was drained. I now asked him to picture himself standing before the Lord as we did at the beginning. Then I asked him to re-feel the deep anger he had towards his mom. He tried but couldn't. Then I encouraged him to thank the Lord for healing that part of his life. I learned he had many more people to process but for now he was at peace regarding his mom.

There was one more issue that needed to be addressed. In the aftermath of his mother's sin were the lies he had come to believe. Lies perpetrate anger and rob you of peace.

RENOUNCE THE LIES

In whatever environment you and I grow up, we tend to think is normal. Solomon said it this way, "There is a way that seems right to a man but its end is the way of death" (Prov. 14:12).

The parenting that Jeff received was very dysfunctional. That was one issue. But with that dysfunction, Satan injected lies into his belief system. For Jeff it was going to be quite a task to identify lies attached to his mother's sin and replace them with truth. This goes beyond merely forgiving the sin.

The first lie he identified was that he was responsible for his mother's ultimate happiness. Each of us is responsible for our own happiness which must come from our personal relationship with the Lord Jesus Christ. The Apostle Paul put it this way, "For me to live is Christ, and to die is gain" (Phil. 1:21). Jeff's mother made him her God-substitute though she still was very active in church. She depended on Jeff for what she should only expect from the Lord Jesus.

In prayer, Jeff firmly renounced the lie that he was ultimately responsible to make his mother happy. He is responsible to love, respect and honor her. But he resigned the ultimate responsibility to meet her spiritual and emotional needs.

Jeff also had to renounce the lie that his mother was totally responsible for *his* happiness. That was a hard shift to make. He affirmed aloud that he was responsible for his own well-being and that he must now look to the Lord Jesus as the ultimate source for his mental, emotional and spiritual well-being. Both Jeff and his mom had become emotionally enmeshed. It took a concerted effort to break free and reestablish a healthy relationship centered around the Lord Jesus and not on each other.

The second lie Jeff dealt with was performance-based acceptance. He renounced that lie and replaced it with the truth that he is accepted by God through his relationship with the Lord Jesus Christ (Eph. 1:6). He is now free to live a godly life *because* he is totally accepted in Christ rather than striving to live a godly life in order to *get* God to accept him. One comes from a heart of appreciation; the other comes from a desperate attempt to be accepted.

Finally he had to renounce the lie that emotions, including anger, are wrong. Emotions in themselves are not wrong but to act them out in a sinful way is wrong. Now Jeff gives himself permission to feel the anger and asks the Lord for its source. His anger acts like a friend who reveals a need, in this case an offense that needs to be forgiven. He now knows what to do and why. He is experiencing greater peace himself and with his mom.

This process did not instantly relieve all their problems. Jeff's changes caused his mother to make some changes that she did not want to make. With the issues regarding his mother settled, many other issues surfaced. In fact he got in touch with other reservoirs of anger. We are still picking them off one at a time.

Over the years I have watched many like Jeff who were trapped in the blazing inferno of rage become released and freed once and for all. Do these "released ones" ever get angry again? Sure. Anger is a normal emotion. But now they are able to deal with current sources of anger at a much lower level of intensity.

Rage is anger intensity at a nine or ten on a scale with ten being high. God's plan for Jeff was to take his rage from ten down to zero as it related to a very significant person in his life, his mother.

God has given to Jeff, and to you, everything needed for life and godliness (II Peter 1:3). That includes tools to work through the gut wrenching hurts of life. God does not want you just to manage your anger or rage. He is clear on this point. "Let *all* bitterness and wrath (rage) and anger ... be put away from you ..." (Eph. 4:32).

One significant process Jeff is experiencing at age 20 that he did not accomplish during his adolescent years, is growing up emotionally! The beautiful part is that he has a great start now and it will not take another 20 years to catch up. He can be a man now and begin to experience God's peace in his home.

ANGER REDUCTION KEYS

1. Decide to implement God's anger reduction plan for your life.
2. Give yourself permission to feel your anger.
3. Use your anger to identify the hurts and those who hurt you.
4. Confess their sin to the Lord without minimizing it.
5. Acknowledge God's responsibility for exacting any revenge.
6. Send the offense and offender over to the Lord Jesus Christ.
7. Confess your own sin to God and receive His forgiveness.
8. Accept upon yourself the consequences of other's sin against you.
9. Convert all losses into a beneficial gain.
10. Identify and renounce all lies and replace them with affirmations of truth.
11. Take responsibility for your own emotional, mental and spiritual well-being before the Lord.

SMALL GROUP DISCUSSION QUESTIONS

1. What patterns from your past do you need to work on?
2. What have others observed in you that indicates a need in your life?
3. What fears prevent you from dealing with a past or present hurtful situation?
4. How were emotions handled in your birth family and how have they been acted out in your own relationships?
5. How do you visualize using anger as a benefit in your life?
6. What dependent relationships have you experienced and how did you correct them? How has your life been different because of this change?
7. What were the hardest offenses you had to forgive and how did you do it? What was the result in you, in others?
8. What were some of the lies you believed early in life? How did you discover them? What did you do about them? What difference did it make in you and in other relationships?
9. What are some of the losses you have had to accept in life? How did you do it? How has acceptance of your losses influenced your life?
10. How have you been able to use past hurts in life to help others?

CHAPTER 13

IRRESPONSIBILITY, FAILURE TO ADDRESS ANGER

Nothing can make you feel more helpless than a conflict in an important relationship. Whether it is between a parent, child, spouse, boyfriend, girlfriend, in-law or an ex-spouse. The stress of a conflict usually extends to work, church, friends, clubs and/ or sports. Nothing is exempt. This stress is a notifier. Something needs to be done, but what?

NUMBER ONE QUESTION

Regardless of the nature of the conflict, the number one question most frequently asked is, "What can I do?" What can I do about my husband's outbursts of anger, my wife's yelling, my daughter's tantrums, the coach's temper, my in-law's sarcasm?

Every effort has proven fruitless so far. Anger reigns and relationships are ruined. Frustration stares you in the face. It looks hopeless. You would like to leave. You still have to live, work, or serve with the angry person. What can you do?

Each year as I read through the Bible I repeatedly see four non-optional keys in working through any relational problem. They are not complicated. If followed they can bring peace. If ignored they will inevitably result in further conflict, hurt, alienation, separation or divorce. These four keys served as the backdrop of our book, *You Can Work It Out*.

- Identify what is happening in the relationship.
- Assign responsibility for all the parts of the conflict.
- Assume responsibility that is legitimately assigned.
- Fulfill all assigned and assumed responsibility.

PART I: IDENTIFY WHAT IS HAPPENING

An important biblical principle comes into play by implementing this first key. *God only gives grace for the truth.* The Apostle John explained that the Lord Jesus Christ came to reconcile man to God on the basis of grace and truth. "And the Word became flesh, and dwelt among us...full of grace and truth" (John 1:14).

God never gives grace for denial. What is Christian denial? It is denying God access to a hurt that He wants to heal for your benefit and His glory. Life will never work for you with God factored out of your trials. He has a specific purpose for all of them (I Cor. 1:4; James 1:2-3).

Denial was the norm in the Laodicean church located in Asia Minor or present day Turkey. This church was one of seven selected by God to receive a personal letter from Him, penned by the Apostle John. In essence God employed a human word picture of being so nauseated that He is about to vomit (Rev. 3:16). What kind of behavior in the church caused God to feel this way? Here is what the church was thinking.

"Because you say, 'I am rich and have become wealthy and have *need of nothing.*'" That's total denial. Then God holds up the mirror of truth and declares, "and (you) do not know that you are wretched, miserable, poor, blind and naked" (Rev. 3:17).

He counsels them to acknowledge their needs and come to Him to get those needs met (Rev. 3:18). In fact He pictures Himself standing outside of their lives seeking access to their wounded hearts. "Behold I stand at the door and knock. If anyone hears my voice and opens the door, I will come into him and dine with him and he with Me" (Rev. 3:20). For the record, God is not talking here to unbelievers but to believers who may have denied Him access. There are at least four reasons you may not want to answer the door and honestly look at the truth, either in yourself or others.

1. A REALITY YOU DO NOT WANT TO ACKNOWLEDGE

Greg had raised four boys alone and had two daughters still at home. One daughter was a middle school student with a major anger problem. It did not take long to discover that his daughter was displaying the same kind and intensity of anger he used in parenting. When she asked him why *she* couldn't respond in anger like he did, he said, "Well, I'm 42." He felt as an adult he could legitimately vent his anger with impunity but it was not okay for her to do it.

Greg justified his anger by reminding me he was Italian. I clearly reminded him that God never excuses sin on the grounds of one's nationality. God's Word is applicable to every culture and gender (Gal. 3:28). Greg tenaciously held onto his feeling that his anger was justifiable. Why? If he acknowledged he had an anger problem he would have to take the responsibility to deal with it.

Cindy's husband was an angry controller. She would resist any positive suggestions to deal with her husband's anger. Why? For two reasons: first, she was emotionally dependent on him and was afraid he would leave her and second, if she took any steps to deal with his anger, she feared his rejection.

Psychiatrists, Dr. Frank Minirth and Dr. Paul Meier, described this pattern in *Love is a Choice* as emotional dependence or co-dependence. It is an addiction to people, behavior or things

(*Love Is a Choice*, p.11). We described co-dependence in chapter 3 as making one human act in the place of God on another's behalf. It is making another human totally responsible for your happiness and ultimate security. Co-dependence is a deceptive effort to control your feelings of fear by attempting to control people, things and circumstances.

Cindy justified her husband's anger until he assaulted her 20 year old daughter and was arrested for it. Now she was willing to acknowledge the reality that she and her family were in an emotionally abusive situation. No peace was going to come to her home until the reality of what was taking place was finally acknowledged and dealt with. There is another reason it is hard to honestly identify what is taking place in a relationship.

2. FEELINGS YOU MAY NOT WANT TO FEEL

Sally made every effort to keep all her feelings totally under control. She shared with me how hurt she felt that her church elder husband was having an emotional affair with a young woman living in their home that they were attempting to help. She described all the things he was doing with the young woman and her children to the exclusion of her and their own children.

Sally kept saying to me that she was just frustrated.

"You mean angry," I suggested. "No, I'm frustrated," she countered. "Are you sure you are just frustrated?" probing further. "Okay...Yes ...I'm...Yeah, I'm angry. No, I'm really ticked!"

Her face turned red with both shame and embarrassment. She was taught all her life do not sin by being angry instead of be angry and sin not (Eph. 4:26). But once Sally was able to feel her anger we were able to use it to compile a list of her husband's offenses. We then spent a significant time in prayer forgiving and releasing him.

There is a reason you may not want to feel a particularly painful emotion. It might overwhelm you. One of Satan's biggest lies is that you *can* feel or re-feel a hurtful emotion so intense that God cannot comfort you. The Apostle Paul made it clear that God promises to comfort you, giving you hope and strength in all your affliction so that you may be able to comfort those in *any* affliction with the comfort that you yourself are comforted by God (II Cor. 1:4). True, it may hurt, but equally true, you need never experience any pain in a comfortless vacuum. Peace will come to your home when you take the responsibility to use your emotions and trace them back to their source.

3. A Responsibility You do Not Want to Assume

What would happen if Greg honestly admitted that he had an anger problem? He would be obligated to address and correct it. This is also the number one reason you may not want to look honestly at a conflict. If you admit to yourself that your boyfriend, husband, or son is addicted to pornography, you may not want to take responsible steps for fear of personal loss. When your fear prevents you from taking responsible action it is called enabling.

Enabling is allowing another person to continue in irresponsible behavior out of fear you may suffer loss if you take responsible steps to correct it. Enabling is never done for the benefit of another. It is only done to protect yourself. It avoids the "tough love" decisions. I prefer to say enabling prevents you from making *responsible* decisions. You can stay in denial, take no action and resist God's grace or step out of denial and experience God's grace and blessing. Remember, God does not heal denial. Why? He is on the "outside" of your conflict wanting to come in with His healing grace and peace. He is not going to shove it under your closed door.

You may be avoiding the need to either ask or grant forgiveness or admit you are controlling out of fear. You may have to face your favoritism, criticism, selfishness, impatience or perfectionism. You may have been a classic blame shifter to avoid personal responsibility.

Honestly identifying what is happening in the conflict means you will take full responsibility for your own words, actions and attitudes. It can also mean you need to stop taking responsibility for other's words, actions and attitudes. Yet, there is another reason you may be reluctant to admit what is taking place.

4. A MOTIVE YOU MAY NOT WANT TO ACKNOWLEDGE

Selfishness is the root of inappropriate anger. One of the major sources of anger results when your *will* is blocked.

Unhealthy anger attempts to change someone, to control them or to get them to do what you want. Anger can also be used to manipulate and avoid responsibility. At the root of this anger are selfish motives, not Christ-like maturity. Unhealthy anger always fails to produce the righteousness of God (James 1:20). It is hard to honestly identify what you are doing because you may have to acknowledge a selfish motive and take responsibility for your actions.

START WITH AN HONEST X-RAY

Why is it an important first step to honestly identify what is happening in the conflict? For the same reason a skilled orthopedic surgeon will not perform corrective surgery until he has had an opportunity to examine a clear set of x-rays.

When I fell off a painting scaffold and landed on my elbow I thought I had merely broken my arm. I suggested to the doctor that he put a cast on it and I would be on my way. It was then he held up my x-rays, pointing out why I would need surgery. I had succeeded in pulverizing my elbow. I was not willing to submit to surgery until I saw with my own eyes the extent of the damage.

Much advice is rejected and good counsel is ignored by those who fail to accept the relationship x-ray. That's why I am sparing with advice until the listener is convinced of the need. "He who corrects a scoffer gets shame for himself. And he who rebukes a wicked man only harms himself" (Prov.9:7). The mocker is unteachable and denies the x-ray of his life. He lashes out in anger and verbal abuse, refusing to admit his own need.

If over-protective parents do not see that they are micro-managing their children out of fear, they will resist, minimize or reject any steps to address their fear. If a controller fails to see the connection between his need to control and his fear of loss, hurt or abandonment, he will reject any suggestion that does *not* allow him to control. If an anger-managed person does not honestly acknowledge the source of his anger, any anger management skills are only doomed to fail. If a perfectionist does not acknowledge the guilt, shame and fear driving his perfectionism, he will not take the necessary steps to address them.

The following simple project has given many people hope for peace in their relationships even before any change ever takes place.

THE "A TO B" PROJECT

Every relationship, organization, club, business or team can utilize this basic concept. It involves asking two simple questions: Where are you AT and where do you want to BE? I have taken every possible relationship problem and asked these two simple questions and have been pleasantly surprised each time with the results. How does this work? Ask yourself what is honestly taking place or where are you at now in the relationship? Make a list but do *not* identify who is doing what. A list of the actions or attitudes being displayed might look something like this:

AT
Criticism
Yelling
Pouting
Apathy
Controlling
Cussing
Name calling
Favoritism
Perfectionism
Disrespect
Insensitivity
Anger
Fear

After getting as exhaustive a list as possible, I ask if there is anything else. When there is agreement that this list sums it up, I then ask the second simple question, "Where do you want to BE?" Usually it is the direct opposite of where they are AT.

AT	**BE**
Critical	Affirming
Yelling	Talking
Withdrawing	Engaging
Apathetic	Caring
Controlling	Relaxed

Cussing	Blessing
Name calling	Honoring
Favoritism	Impartiality
Perfectionism	Balanced
Disrespectful	Respectful
Insensitive	Sensitive
Angry	Forgiving
Fearful	Trusting

Now the crucial question, "Do you really want to go from where you are *at* to where you said you want to *be*? I wish every person who completed this exercise said, "Yes!" But some people are addicted to their misery. Why? It is comfortable, predictable and all they have known. They fear going through the process of change even though they acknowledge where they should be. But for the most part the response is very encouraging. It is the first time for many to take a look at where they are *at* and where they can *be*. Now they feel someone can coach them through the changes and experience a much better quality of life.

After one couple made this x-ray of their relationship they felt they learned more in this one exercise than in many months of marriage counseling with another counselor. Why? They made an honest assessment of what was working and what was not working in their relationship. Now they have hope because they could visualize the possibility of a much better relationship.

You can experience God's peace in any difficult relationship when you realistically admit exactly what is taking place that makes it so painful. Then, determine where you want to be. Finally, decide you are willing to go from where you are *at* to where you want to *be*. This process is only the first step. The second step can be hard on pride but great for peace.

PART II. ASSIGN RESPONSIBILITY FOR ALL THE PARTS OF THE CONFLICT

When our book, *You Can Work It Out,* was first published, the subtitle carried the real punch, "*The Power of Personal Responsibility in Restoring Relationships.*" Romans 12:18 is at the heart of that book. What brings the possibility of peace in any relationship? "If possible so far as it depends on you, be at peace with all men" (Rom. 12:18).

If failing to take an honest x-ray of the relationship is one of the top reasons for counseling failure, then failing to assign responsibility is right next to it. Assigning responsibility is exactly what Paul meant by, "As much as it depends on you" (Rom. 12:18).

I have referred to this assigning concept as "circles of responsibilities." The apostle could very well have said, "If possible, as much as it lies within your circle of responsibility, be at peace with all men."

God's peace will elude any relationship if each person fails to assign what is legitimately in their own circle of responsibility. How is this done? First, draw a circle for each person in the relationship. Then go down the "At" list of anger producing components and ask, "Who is responsible for what?" Assign each item on the list to the one to whom it belongs. You might ask, "Who is being critical?" Then write "critical" in their circle. Who is doing the yelling? Write the word "yelling" in that person's circle.

When I met with Greg concerning his angry daughter I asked if he was using his anger to change, control or manipulate her. After minimizing his anger he finally came around to accepting the responsibility for his anger and listed it in his circle.

Jesus conveyed the same concept of personal responsibility, "Do not judge so that you will not be judged. For in the way you judge, you will be judged, and by your standard of measure, it will be measured to you. Why do you look at the speck that is in your brother's eye (or circle of responsibility), but do not notice the log that is in your own eye (or in your circle)? Or how can you say to your brother, 'Let me take the speck out of your eye,' and behold, the log is in your own eye? You hypocrite, first take the log out of your own eye, and then you will see clearly to take the speck out of your brother's eye" (Matt. 7:1-5).

Jesus never said you could not help correct another person. He simply said by removing the beam in your own eye (dealing with what is in your own circle of responsibility) you will see clearly how to take out the speck in another's eye. In fact, he may be more open to your help after you have dealt with your own circle of responsibility.

The phrase, "If possible" hints of a possible reality. It means you can do everything in your circle of responsibility and have the whole thing blow up in your face. Remember, Jesus did everything right in direct obedience to His Heavenly Father and His own people killed Him (John 1:11), but when you suffer for doing the right thing you become highly favored in God's eyes (I Pet. 2:20).

Identifying and assigning responsibilities are logical. But the third step of releasing God's power into your home or relationship may not be as obvious. It should be implied in the second step but much peace eludes our relationships because of failure in this crucial next step.

PART III. ASSUME RESPONSIBILITY THAT IS LEGITIMATELY ASSIGNED

Assigning and assuming responsibilities are related yet different. You can assign something for someone to do but that does not mean they assumed what has been assigned. You can tell your children to go clean up their room. Upon inspecting their room an hour later you discover it has not been touched. Why? You assigned, they failed to assume.

After I have each person in a conflict list what is in their circle of responsibility, I then ask a very pointed question, "Do you assume full responsibility to correct what is in your own circle and to get any appropriate help you need to accomplish it?" I have traced my personal failure to help someone back to my neglect in getting a firm commitment up front that he *will* assume full responsibility for his stuff.

ASSUME YOUR OWN RESPONSIBILITY

Margaret was one of the most caring, gentle, selfless and diligent women I have ever met. What was this woman in her 40's doing in my office? She was headed for a breakdown. Margaret embodied all five of the reasons people assume responsibility that is not theirs.

KEEP THE PEACE

First, she wanted to keep peace with her husband, Earl. If anything went wrong in the home or with the kids he made it clear it was her fault. She learned early from her compliant mother that if you assume all the responsibility, people will not get mad at you. To keep Earl from getting angry she assumed responsibility for everything and everyone. Twenty-six years later Earl was still getting mad. The kids were never held responsible for their behavior so they didn't respect her. The life of peace she sought was turning into chaos around her.

AVOID GUILT

Margaret assumed responsibility for almost everything to avoid feelings of guilt. If Earl was unhappy it must have been something she did or failed to do. She taught the family that they could get her to do anything if they just applied a tourniquet of guilt to her conscience.

The word "guilt" means "worthy of blame." Guilt is not a bad word. What Margaret failed to do was to ask herself one of the most important questions a guilt driven person should ask, "Am I worthy of blame?" Or to put it another way, "Am I responsible for Earl's or the kids' total happiness?"

Since true guilt and false guilt *feel* the same, you must train yourself to test your emotions with truth or reality. If you fail to do this consistently you will wrongfully assume responsibility for others' behavior and happiness and live in a dungeon of self-condemnation and guilt.

GAIN ACCEPTANCE

Because Margaret was raised on a steady diet of conditional acceptance she gladly assumed responsibility that was not hers, hoping to gain that acceptance. However, assuming others' responsibilities failed to bring the acceptance she sought. Usually it breeds disdain that comes out in many forms of disrespect.

AVOID REJECTION

Margaret became an over-responsible person to avoid rejection. Rejection is one of the most painful emotions you can feel. When someone rejects you they devalue your worth and figuratively cast you aside.

Rejection had sliced its way deeply into Margaret's heart as an unwanted third child. Her two older sisters were all her parents planned for. Then came Margaret, the surprise. She was tolerated, never treasured. She came into her marriage starved for acceptance and affection at any cost.

Margaret reasoned that by holding no one responsible for their actions and assuming everyone's responsibility, she would get acceptance and avoid rejection. Today she cries in my office, rejected by all, and bitter at God. She honestly believed God required her to assume all the responsibility.

If you are attempting to avoid rejection by being over-responsible mark your calendar. The day you cease to assume others' responsibilities you can expect their rejection.

TRY TO FIX IT

Margaret naively believed that if it was her fault she could fix whatever was broken in the relationship. But no one is ever helped who is not allowed to assume their own circle of responsibility.

National newscasters referred to the 90's as the decade of no responsibility. Since no one was responsible for anything nothing got fixed. It was the decade of unfinished business. The years of the new millennium are ones of picking up the pieces. That is just what Margaret was doing. It was the pieces of her own life.

Psychologists Townsend and Cloud's book, *Boundaries*, became a national best-seller and received the honored Gold Medallion Award. Why? They demonstrated from Scripture and psychology the importance of personal responsibility and how it works in everyday relationships. They view boundaries as the healthy limits you establish in what you allow others to impose on you and what you impose on yourself. I call it circles of responsibilities. *Boundaries* view personal responsibility from the outside in. Circles of responsibilities view the same concept from the inside out. God will only give you grace and power for what is in your circle.

STAY IN YOUR OWN CIRCLE

Doctor Rich called me early one morning. His voice was shaky. Things were going from bad to worse with his wife and kids. His wife came from a very abusive home. She was now acting out on him and the four kids the same patterns she experienced in her birth home. She hated the kids and Rich could do nothing right. To her credit she was getting professional help and so was Rich.

Rich began slowly, "I know I have not responded well many times to my wife. I've confessed it and asked forgiveness. She just told me the kids and I have ruined her life and she wants a divorce." Then in a soft almost pleading voice he said, "I've tried so hard . . . is God going to judge me for what she does if she goes through with this?"

Over the next few minutes we reviewed what had been happening and who was responsible for what. We redefined what was in each member of the family's circle of responsibilities. Then I asked him, "Did you assume full responsibility for what was in your own circle?" "Yeah" came a weak but honest reply.

I assured him, "God will only hold you accountable for what is in your circle of responsibility." Rich broke down in tears. I waited. God's Spirit was taking that truth deep into his heart. I began slowly quoting II Corinthians 5:10: "For we must all appear before the judgment seat of Christ, that each one may be recompensed for his deeds in the body, according to what he has done, whether good or bad."

I was quick to remind him that salvation is not the issue here. Salvation is by faith and is a free gift (Eph. 2:8-9). Only the deeds of the believer will be evaluated. I encouraged him that God would never hold him responsible for his wife's words, actions or attitudes. Just his and his alone. This one truth has given many people extra energy to focus on their own circle and trust God for the rest.

God does not bless those who merely identify what is not working in a relationship. He doesn't even bless those who have accurately assigned responsibility. Surprisingly, He does not even bless those who step up to the plate and assume their own circle of responsibility. There is something else. Without it no blessing or peace is going to come.

PART IV. FULFILL RESPONSIBILITIES

For years, as a pastor, I naively believed that if I could get people to honestly admit what was happening in a conflict, assign responsibility and get them to assume their responsibilities, I was home free. The rest was up to them.

I failed to fully understand the ways of God in restoring relationships until God drove home this one simple truth. "But prove yourselves doers of the Word, and not merely hearers who delude themselves," (James 1:22). James removes any confusion, "But one who looks intently at the perfect law, the law of liberty, and abides by it, not having become a forgetful hearer but an effectual doer (fulfiller), this man will be blessed in what he does" (James 1:25).

When people are still in conflict after extensive counseling, one question I ask is, "Are each of you fulfilling what is in your own circle of responsibility?" Many people expect a change without making any change. They may complain that counseling did not work. What is my response? "Please tell me what ways of God you tried that did not work." The usual response is, "I don't know," which can be a form of denial or can mean, "I know but I'm not going to admit it to you."

Often people will tell me they just had a big blow up and feel they are back to square one. When I ask if they used the Scriptural tools they had been learning, invariably they admit they did not. This reflects the law of insanity, rephrased, "If you always do what you have always done, you'll always get what you have always gotten." The Apostle Paul said it this way, "Whatever a man sows, that he will also reap" (Gal. 6:7). Plant corn, get corn. Sow beans, get beans. Sow obedience, reap blessing. You will reap at least ten benefits by fulfilling your circle of responsibility.

1. It will keep you focused.
2. It will give you a clear purpose.
3. It will allow you to measure your progress.
4. You will experience a greater security.
5. Anxiety will be greatly reduced.
6. There will be a reduction in tension.
7. Conflict will be reduced.
8. Relationships may get rebuilt.
9. You will have a powerful witness.
10. There will be a greater sense of inner peace.

This is just a start. There is incredible power in identifying, assigning, assuming and fulfilling your own circle of responsibility. You are able to take back the control, direction, blessing and fulfillment in your own life. If you are the only one in your life who ever changes, you will hear the most exciting words from an awesome God, "... well done, good and faithful servant" (Matt. 25:21).

Flying home from California I read the following caption under a beautifully matted picture of a mature oak tree silhouetted against a bright orange sunset. "This is the beginning of a new day. You have been given this day to use as you will. You can waste it or you can use it for good. What you do today is important because you are exchanging a day of your life for it. When tomorrow comes, this day is gone forever: in its place is something that you have left behind...let it be something good."

What is one of the greatest legacies you could leave behind? The change you have made in yourself and help make in others because of the seeds of peace you have sown (James 3:18).

Use emotions like anger and fear to discover needs, then, seek to meet them with all your heart. This could just be the doorway to bringing God's peace into your home.

A fellow peacemaker,
Chuck Lynch

ANGER REDUCTION KEYS

1. Honestly identify what is happening in a relationship to cause anger and frustration.
2. Boldly face any emotion, responsibility or motive you have been avoiding.
3. Evaluate where you are *at* and where you want to *be*, then, take responsible steps to get there.
4. Assign responsibility for all the parts of a conflict.
5. Assume responsibility that is legitimately yours.
6. Avoid assuming others' responsibilities.
7. Fulfill all your assigned and assumed responsibilities.

SMALL GROUP DISCUSSION QUESTIONS

1. Briefly describe a relational conflict that brought you to your wit's end. What were the attempts you made to correct it?

2. What are the reasons you have not honestly faced a difficult situation? What did you have to do before you could face it? Did someone help you? How did they help you?

3. What negative emotions have you faced in life and how were you able to deal with them?

4. What are some of the most difficult responsibilities you have had to assume? Why were they hard? How did you finally come to assume them?

5. How did you take an honest x-ray of your life (or situation)? How was it helpful?

6. What problems have you had getting others to assume their responsibility in a conflict? What has worked or not worked for you?

7. Share a time that you did the right thing and it blew up in your face. How did you respond? What did God teach you through it?

8. Describe how others attempted to get you to assume their responsibilities. How did you respond to them? What was their response?

9. Share a time when you had to stand alone in fulfilling your circle of responsibilities. What effect did it have on those around you? What did God teach you through it?

BIBLIOGRAPHY

Beattie, Melody. *Co-dependent No More.* New York: Harper and Row Publishing, 1987.

Burchette, Dave. *When Bad Christians Happen to Good People.* Colorado Springs: Water Brook Press, 2002.

Carter, Less. *Good and Angry.* Grand Rapids: Baker, 1983.

Chapman, Gary. *The Five Love Languages.* Chicago: Northfield Publishing, 1992.

Chapman, Gary. *The Other Side of Love.* Chicago: Moody, 1999.

Cloud, Henry & John Townsend. *Boundaries.* Grand Rapids: Zondervan Publishing House, 1992.

Crabb, Larry. *The Silence of Adam.* Grand Rapids: Zondervan Publishing House, 1995.

Dobson, James. *Dare to Discipline.* Wheaton: Tyndale House Publishing, 1992.

Enroth, Ronald. *Churches That Abuse.*

Friel, John. *Adult Children, the Secrets of Dysfunctional Families.* Deerfield Beach: Health Communications, 1988.

Friel, John & Linda. *The Seven Worst Things.* Deerfield Beach: Health Communications, 1999.

Hemfelt, Robert & Warren, Paul. *Kids Who Carry Our Pain.* Nashville: Thomas Nelson Publishing, 1990.

Hughes, Selwyn. *Helping People Through Their Problems.* Minneapolis: Bethany House, 1981.

Learner, Harriet. *The Dance of Anger.* New York: Harper and Row Publishing, 1985.

Lynch, Chuck. *I Should Forgive, But. . .* Nashville: Word Publishing, 1998.

Lynch, Chuck. *You Can Work It Out.* Nashville: Word Publishing, 1999.

Minirth, Frank & Paul Meier. *Love is a Choice.* Nashville: Thomas Nelson Publishing, 1989.

Oliver, Gary & Norman H. Wright. *Raising Kids to Love Jesus.* Ventura: Regal, 1999.

Rinck, Margaret. *Christian Men Who Hate Women.* Grand Rapids: Zondervan Publishing House, 1990.

Smalley, Gary. *The Key to Your Child's Heart.* Nashville: Word Publishing, 1984.

Stack, Debi. *Martha to the Max.* Chicago: Moody Press, 2000.

Stoop, David & Arterburn, Stephen. *The Angry Man.* Nashville: Word Publishing, 1991.

Stoop, David. *What Is He So Angry About?* Nashville: Word Publishing,

Worthen, Anita & Bob Davies. *Someone I Love is Gay.* Downers Grove: Inter Varsity Press, 1996.

Wright, H. Norman. *Crisis Counseling.* San Bernardino: Here's Life Publishing, 1985.

Wright, H. Norman. *Pre-Hysteric Parenting.* Colorado Springs: Faith Parenting, 2001.

Living Foundation Ministries, Inc.
611 NW R.D. Mize Road · Blue Springs, MO 64014
816-229-5000 · website: www.help4living.org